CHAPTERS

PROLOGUE

I met Terry Oliver in Sheffield in 1980. I had just returned to the casino, where I was trained to become a croupier, after working in Brighton for eight months. Terry had just returned to Sheffield after doing a stint in the London casinos.

I was a young and naive twenty one year old. Five foot ten, eight stone, pale skin and ginger. Terry was about the same age and height. But that's where the similarity ended. He was heavier built with a dark complexion to match his thick black hair and dark eyes. He was a lot more confident than I was and a lot more self-assured when it came to chatting up the birds.

Terry and I hit it off straight away. We both smoked hash, liked a drink or two and we both played backgammon. We did a lot of double shifts together in the casino. Between shifts we'd get an hour off so together we'd go on a mini pub crawl smoking a joint between each pub. We drove the inspectors and the pit bosses crazy returning to work the night shift intoxicated and stoned. Fortunately we were both good at our job.

One evening in May of 1981 Terry and I were in the pub having a relaxing drink after working a day shift when he asked me if I fancied going to work in Amsterdam. All I knew about Amsterdam was that dope was legal and every window had a hooker in it. I didn't know anything about the gambling scene in Holland. Neither did Terry, but he did have friends over there. His friend Dave from London had phoned Terry and told him to come on over.

The casinos were illegal, the money was good and there was plenty of work to be had. It wasn't a difficult decision to make. We booked a week's holiday, bought two return tickets on the ferry from Harwich to the Hoek of Holland, packed our bags and set off on our great adventure.

CHAPTER ONE
WE ARRIVE
12th JULY 1981

Terry and I walked out of Amsterdam's railway station into a bright July sunny morning. We both flinched as the intensity of the sun burned into our eyes. Being croupiers we weren't used to dazzling daylight. We'd sailed overnight from Harwich to the Hoek of Holland. We hadn't slept. Terry had spent most of the journey trying to convert a party of black Americans to Communism. I'd opened the litre bottle of Johnny Walker Black Label whisky I'd bought duty free and between Terry, myself and the Americans that could keep up, we polished the bottle off before we arrived in Holland. We were both tired and drunk when we walked out into that sunshine, but we were both looking forward to the adventure that lay before us.

Terry had arranged for his friend Dave to pick us up outside the station, but he wasn't to be seen. We had Dave's telephone number so Terry gave him a call from one of the numerous telephone boxes outside the station. No answer. Terry hung up and three twenty five cent coins were returned to us. We'd only put in one.

We went to another phone box and rang Dave again. There was still no answer. Terry hung up and again seventy five cents were returned to us. We'd made two phone calls and already we were one guilder in profit. Armed with plenty of twenty five cent coins Terry and I hit every phone box ringing Dave, hoping he wouldn't answer.

Terry finally got through to Dave who told us he was on his way. While we waited and knowing Dave wasn't at home Terry and I went from phone to phone ringing his number and collecting our fifty cents profit each time. By the time Dave arrived about twenty minutes later in his beat up yellow VW Beetle we were showing a healthy profit, our pockets bulging with twenty five cent coins. We threw our bags in the boot and he whisked us off to his flat on the outskirts of town.

The flat was large, airy and well furnished. Coming from an English bedsit this place was luxurious. Dave showed us around the flat and when he got to his bedroom he opened the door and introduced us to Cathy, his girl friend. They'd both worked the previous night shift and Cathy was trying to get some sleep. She raised her head from the pillow, said hello then went back to sleep. Terry and Cathy had met before in London. With all those phone calls we had been making we must have driven Cathy round the bend but she never said anything about them.

Terry and I may have been up all night drinking whisky, but we were no longer tired. The sights and sounds and the smell of the city had got us buzzing with excitement. Dave was fully awake and wanting to leave Cathy to get some sleep he drove us out to the Flevoparkbad, one of Amsterdam's open air swimming pools on the Zeeburgerdijk in the east of the city. We lay down on the newly cut grass with our shirts off, drinking cold Heinekens, toking on a grass joint and perving at the Dutch girls wandering about in their bikinis. Dave filled us in on the city in general and the work situation in the casinos. He told us he would take us to the casino where he worked later that evening to see if we could get a job. After a couple of hours laying in the sun drinking cold beers we returned to the flat.

I didn't know about Terry, but the lack of sleep, several cold beers and exposure to bright sunshine was beginning to catch up with me. With Dave's permission I took a shower and soon found out I'd caught the sun. My chest, back, arms and face were bright red and on fire. After drying myself off I went into the second double bedroom to get dressed and it was there that I met Paul, Dave's flat mate. I was bouncing up and down on his double bed in my underpants trying to put on a clean pair of socks when he walked in. I introduced myself and when I'd finished dressing we went into the living room where Paul introduced me to his girlfriend and flat mate Evelyn.

Paul, Eve, Cathy and Dave all worked in the Cabala and it was their day off. The afternoon drifted by in a haze of marijuana smoke and more cold cans of Heineken. Come early evening with Cathy having got up, showered, dressed and looking a million dollars we all waited for Terry to make himself presentable. Paul and Eve were staying in for the evening. Once Terry was ready we headed into the city for a much needed bite to eat. Terry and I were both starving by now. I can't remember where we went to eat. It must have been around eleven o'clock later that night when Dave and Cathy took us to the Cabala casino.

The Cabala was situated in the Red Light district on the Oudezijds Achterburgwal. I'd never seen anything like it. The canals were lined with hookers sitting in windows with their red lights, some on, some off. Everywhere I looked there were neon lights advertising hookers, bars, sex shops and clubs showing live sex shows. The place was buzzing with business.

Dave led us into the Cabala casino. It was a busy night. The tables were in full swing and there was a lot of money changing hands. Dave spoke to someone, probably a manager, and Terry and I were led out back to a quieter room and both given a table test. We passed with flying colours but, we were told that the Cabala was fully staffed and they weren't hiring. It was a bit disconcerting as Terry had insisted all along that there was plenty of work for both of us. Dave must have noticed my mood because he told me not to worry, there were plenty of casinos in town and he guaranteed we would get a job.

We left the Cabala. Dave wanted to take us out on the town. Terry was up for it but I was beginning to feel the effects of a long day and sunburn. It was a hot night but I was shivering and I just wanted to sleep. Dave gave me directions to a taxi rank. I left them to it and wandered off past all the hookers and the bright neon lights. It was my first night in Amsterdam and I was alone. I was tired, a bit drunk and stoned, sunburnt and disorientated. Needless to say I didn't go too far before I doubled back to the Cabala. The doorman remembered me. I told him I'd got lost and he kindly ordered me a taxi which took me back to the flat. Paul and Eve were still up and they let me in. They got me bedded down and I had my first good nights sleep in Amsterdam.

CHAPTER TWO
THE DAY AFTER THE NIGHT BEFORE

I woke up late morning the next day. My head was throbbing and my skin was on fire. Paul and Eve were in the kitchen making coffee. I got dressed and went to the bathroom to freshen up. Terry, Dave and Cathy were still asleep. No idea what time they got in last night.

I went into the kitchen, Paul handed me a cup of coffee and I lit up a Gitane cigarette. He told me Eve was working that afternoon but he was free and asked me what I wanted to do. I told him I fancied getting some breakfast and going to see the Bulldog Cafe, Amsterdam's most famous 'coffee shop'. Paul thought it was a good plan of action. We finished our coffee and Paul and Eve took me on my first tram ride into the city centre.

The trams in Amsterdam rumble and clatter their way along on tracks in the middle of the roads. They're three or four carriages long and they're painted bright yellow. They looked like giant caterpillars crawling through the city. We got off in Dam Plein and Paul took us to a cafe for a typical Dutch breakfast of ham, eggs and melted cheese on two slices of bread. It was a breakfast I was to both eat and make myself many times whilst I was in Amsterdam.

After breakfast we walked Eve to work. Now that it was daylight and I was sober I was able to get my bearings. The Red Light district looked so different in daylight but it was still full of activity with tourists taking in the sights. The daytime hookers were in the windows. The sex shops were open for trade and the hawkers for the live sex shows were trying to drum up business. "Ten guilders to get in, twenty to get out." They shouted out to the tourists passing by.

We dropped Eve off at the Cabala and Paul and I continued walking through the Red Light district. Paul talked, I stared. He explained how things worked. How much the girls charged for sex. He told me not to take pictures of the hookers as it was strictly forbidden and if I did I would meet the 'entertainments committee', big guys who ran the security throughout the city. He pointed out the local Hells Angels bar. With their motorbikes parked outside in a row and their windows open with the Rolling Stones blasting out, I thought it would be a good place to visit. Paul knew what I was thinking and told me not to go there unless I was invited.

I noticed about fifteen elderly people suddenly appear from nowhere running across one of the bridges. Paul told me that some of the casinos had bingo at different times of the day and all those people were running from one casino to another to catch the next game. It was a regular occurrence and always quiet amusing to watch.

We turned left off the Oudezijds Achterburgwal, crossed a bridge on the Oude Kennissteeg by the Oude Kerk onto the Oudezijds Voorburgwal and there before me was the infamous Bulldog Cafe. I wasn't quiet sure what to expect but from the outside it seemed rather small.

The Bulldog Cafe occupied the ground floor and basement of a typical three storey Dutch house. Its door and window were open, music drifted out onto the street. The exterior of the cafe had recently been painted graffiti style and was bright and becoming for such an establishment. We went inside. There was a bar where you could buy cakes, buns and cookies. Tea, coffee and freshly squeezed orange juice was also on offer. People sat around at tables eating, drinking, reading newspapers and rolling and smoking joints. The air was pungent with the smell of hashish and cannabis. I told Paul I wanted to buy some dope. He took me into the basement which housed another smaller bar with fewer tables, a pinball machine along one wall and a table football game in the middle of the room.

In the corner at the end of the bar sat a man who Paul took me to. I told him I wanted to buy some dope. Opening a bag full of little plastic bags containing different types of hash and grass he asked me what I would like. I'd shifted some gear back home but this was just too much. He had Moroccan, Afghan, Lebanese Red, Lebanese Gold, Paki Black dipped in opium and Nepalese temple balls. He had grass from Jamaica, Nigeria, Columbia and Thailand. Twenty five guilders a bag, the weight depended on the quality. I bought a bag of Afghan hash and a bag of Thai sticks with a packet of Rizlas and a booklet of little cardboard 'roaches'.

We left the Bulldog and continued our wander. Paul took me to the Mata Hari, the other big casino in the Red Light district at the end of the Oudezijds Achterburgwal on the corner of the Korte Niezel. It was already busy with people of all nationalities playing the tables. We asked and found out there weren't any jobs going so we walked back to the Dam Plein.

The Dam Plein was big. At one end it was dominated by the Krasnapolsky Hotel. At the other end, even more imposing, stood the Palace, the official residence of the Queen when she was in town. Trams, taxis, buses, cars, pigeons, buskers and people made the 'Dam' a busy place. Paul pointed out the Kalverstraat, the pedestrian area where all the shops were. We walked down the Rokin to the flower market on the Singel canal by Munt Plein and from there into Rembrandts Plein. We doubled back through the flower market and walked down the Leidsestraat and into the Leidse Plein.

The Leidse Plein area would be where I would end up living the most. This is where the city's other night life went down. Bars, clubs, nightclubs, restaurants, snack bars, cinemas and live music. This is where it all went on.

We were hungry so Paul took me to this snack bar place. Along both walls were these little compartments with food inside them. You chose what you wanted, put in the correct coins and out would come whatever you'd selected. Sausages, chicken and things that were so hot they burnt your mouth, all sorts. First we ordered some chips. This is when I found out that the Dutch loved putting mayonnaise on their chips. Hey I was a convert, still am. We got our coins out, chose an accompaniment to our chips and continued our wander.

Paul pointed out the way to Vondel Park, Amsterdam's biggest park. He showed me the Melkweg on the Lijnbaansgracht opposite the police station and the Paradiso on the Weteringschans, later to become two of my favourite venues for live music. The afternoon was getting on and we had to be home as Cathy and Eve were cooking dinner for us all that night. So we caught a tram and made our way home to the flat.

CHAPTER THREE
WE GET A JOB

After an excellent dinner cooked by Cathy and Eve, Dave drove Terry and I into the city. He'd heard of a job going in one of the casinos. Dave parked the car and we walked to this casino on the Reguliers Dwarsstraat just off the Rembrandts Plein. Dave rang the bell and a short while later the door was opened and we were admitted. It was about eight o'clock at night.

Before us was a wide flight of stairs which took us up to the first floor. At the top we swung a right then a left and we were in the casino. It was just like an apartment that had been converted for the purpose of gambling. In the corner was a round poker table. Next to that sat a couple of slot machines. Down one wall was a bar with a couple of toilets in the end corner. Down the other side of the room was an American roulette table, a blackjack table and a French roulette table.

Terry and I checked the place out while Dave went to speak to someone he obviously knew. Dave came back and introduced us to a guy called Theo, who was one of the bosses. He told us there was one job going and we were going to do a table test. Terry went onto the blackjack table and I went onto the American roulette table. We were dealing to real customers. With the help from this Dutch croupier called Hank we soon picked up on things and just got on with what we both did best.

After about half an hour Dave said goodbye. He had to go back home and get changed, he was working later that evening. An hour later Terry and I were told to change tables. I was now dealing blackjack and Terry was dealing roulette. A table test would normally take twenty to thirty minutes. We'd both been dealing for an hour and a half. We both kept dealing. We both kept taking money. I was beginning to think they were taking the piss and having us working for nothing. An hour later we were both given a break and Theo took us over to the bar and got us both a beer.

Theo was a tall man of average build with short brushed back golden hair and blue eyes. Straight off you could tell he had a wicked sense of humour and the way his eyes kept wandering it was clear he was a ladies man. He came across like a retired porno star from the 1960's. He reminded us there was only one job going. However, as he was impressed with the pair of us we were both hired and would start the next night at ten o'clock and work until six o'clock for twenty five guilders an hour, roughly the equivalent of ten pounds an hour. Theo introduced us to his two partners. Leo, the elder of the three and his nephew Erwin. Theo called Hank over and left him with us.

Hank was the Dutch croupier who had helped us earlier. It was quickly becoming apparent that all Dutch men seemed to be tall with blond hair and blue eyes. He pointed out certain members of staff and briefed us on how things worked. Unlike the Cabala, which was pretty much open to the public the Louis Seize , as the club was known, was illegal hence the security on the door. Hank introduced us to a short fat round geezer called Harry. An Indonesian man with short black frizzy hair, dark brown eyes and a big squashy nose. Harry was about five feet tall and three feet wide. A happy and friendly sort of character. He was the doorman who'd let us in earlier. He explained that Harry was the katvanger (katvanger closely translates as 'front man'). If we got raided we were to tell the police that Harry was the boss, we didn't get paid and we worked for tips which worked out at about a hundred guilders a night.

After a while Terry and I finished our beers. It was getting on for midnight. We said goodnight to Hank and Harry escorted us to the exit. Outside we both lit up a cigarette and just started grinning at each other like maniacs. We were both in work and together at the same place. We decided to celebrate with a drink. We were in the city. We were on our own. It was time to explore the bars around Rembrandts Plein.

We hit a few bars in the Rembrandts Plein and smoked a joint. I decided to show Terry the Bulldog Cafe in the Red Light district. I remembered the way from that afternoons trek with Paul. We wandered round the windows with their neon lights until we came across the Bulldog. I showed Terry around inside and took him to see the man to buy some dope.

I guided Terry out of the Red Light district to the 'Dam'. It was still early, we were still buzzing, so I took him down to the Leidse Plein. A brisk walk down the Leidsestraat and into a busy Leidse Plein. Terry was loving it. He hadn't been here before. The place was lit up with neon lights. There were bars and restaurants everywhere we looked. We spent a couple of hours drinking and observing the human traffic wandering by, then jumped into a taxi and went back to Dave's for some sleep.

CHAPTER FOUR
THE LOUIS SEIZE

Terry and I reported for work at the Louis Seize on our third night in town. Hank came over and introduced us to Chrissie the pit boss. She showed us around, pointing out the staff toilets and the kitchen out back. We were introduced to the black cat that lived in the casino and Chrissie pointed out the office. We popped our heads round the door and said good evening to Leo and Erwin. Leo was sat behind the desk. He was the elder of the three. Short brown mousey hair with his glasses perched on the end of his nose. A nondescript looking man with a razor sharp mind. Erwin was sat on the other side of the desk, he was Leo's nephew. Erwin was a big tall powerful man. He had light sandy hair swept back with piercing blue eyes set in a flat chiselled face but when he smiled he seemed less imposing. Theo was out on the floor keeping his eye on the tables.

Chrissie introduced us to the staff who were working that night. On the French roulette table was Jap, a tall man with a well rounded beer belly, big hands, clear blue eyes and a head of combed back white hair. Opposite him sat Bart, he was related to Leo. Bart was as old as the hills and he looked it. They were both dealing a small game at the time. I'd heard of, but never seen a French roulette table in action before.

On the blackjack table flicking through an English magazine was Liz. She was from Newcastle and had a good old Geordie accent.

She had a shock of long brown curly hair, big brown eyes, which always seemed to twinkle with lust, and a face carved out of granite.

On the roulette table was Valerie, a tall girl with glasses and long blond hair. Next to her, chipping up was Hank who we'd met the night before. Chrissie introduced us to the waitress called Rosie. She was an older lady with black shiny hair. Rosie was from Indonesia and she was drop dead gorgeous. Sat at the bar was a guy called Italian Tony, early forties, short curly grey hair and a cheeky grin. He spoke English with a typical Italian accent. He had something to do with the casino but I never figured out what.

Chrissie allocated Terry to the American roulette table with Hank and I gave Liz a break on the blackjack table. Being new faces in the casino we soon had a game each. Everyone wanted to check out the new boys, see if we were any good. A couple of hours later my table had emptied as I'd cleaned the punters out. I watched Terry on the roulette table which soon after also died out. That was the way the night shifts would be at the Louis Seize. You'd stand around doing nothing for hours then you'd get a sudden burst of some serious action which could go on for two, three, four hours at a time.

During one of our quieter periods I soon found out that Liz liked to play backgammon. I was playing with Liz on the blackjack table and Terry was playing with Hank over on the poker table. Jap and Bart were chatting away with Italian Tony over on the French roulette table. Theo was sat at the bar chatting up some bird and Erwin was sat at the other end talking to Rosie. I looked around and thought this was a nice relaxed and friendly place to work.

We were soon back in action and we continued dealing until we closed at six o'clock. With the punters gone we sat around at the bar drinking beers while Chrissie, Theo and Erwin went out back in the office to empty the drop boxes and count the nights takings. Leo came out of the office and gave me two hundred guilders for my nights wages. Leo thanked everyone for a good nights work. We'd had a good win that night. Terry and I said goodnight to everyone and we walked into the Rembrandts Plein and got a taxi back to Dave's.

CHAPTER FIVE
MY FIRST FLAT

Terry and I had worked two full shifts at the Louis Seize. It was whilst working the second shift that I acquired the nickname of 'Red'. Given to me by Theo. Not because of my ginger hair, but because of the colour of my sunburnt skin. The name stuck and from then on I only answered to the name of Red.

We were working eight hour days for two hundred guilders a shift. Back then that was the equivalent of approximately eighty pounds sterling. Today in 2011 that is the equivalent of two hundred and forty pounds a shift. Double what we were earning back in England and tax free. We realised we couldn't stay at Dave's for too long so we told him we'd move out into a hotel until we had enough money to get a flat.

Dave agreed and drove us to the Village Hotel on the Kerkstraat, close to the Leidse Plein. It was owned and run by a guy called Rudy Kallenbach who just happened to have a vacant room with twin beds. It was a nice room, large and clean with its own bathroom. Terry and I paid a weeks rent and we moved in and made ourselves at home.

Terry and I continued to work the night shift at the Louis Seize. We'd stagger back to the hotel at about eight or nine o'clock in the morning drunk and stoned. We'd sleep all day, get up, eat and go back to work again. The money was beginning to pile up in our pockets. We quickly learnt that we could easily save one hundred guilders a day and still find it difficult to blow the other hundred guilders in a day.

It was whilst working the night shifts that I started to get to know some of our regular customers. Late in the mornings we would get a visit from a group of Chinese punters. One of them was called Pete, he was shorter than me but stockier. He had shoulder length shiny black hair with a thick goatee beard to match. He wore a lot of denim and was always adorned with gold chains and bracelets. On his wrist he wore a diamond encrusted Rolex watch. Pete was a high roller, his pockets were always bulging with cash. He had a habit of standing right next to me when I was dealing and when he was losing he would practice his kick boxing on me. He would let out a torrent of abuse in Dutch and he would hit me on my top left hand thigh with his knee. After Pete had done his money and left I would often end up with a dead leg and in need of a rest to recover. Apart from the physical attacks I did like Pete, he was a good laugh.

Pete was often accompanied by a guy called Sonny. Never over the top in the jewellery department and a lot more serious than Pete. Sonny, like Pete, always seemed to have unlimited supplies of cash on him. He wasn't as easily approachable as Pete but he wasn't a bad lad.

With Pete and Sonny came Chinese Andrew and Alan. Andrew had long black hair, he was clean shaven with a round face and a menacing glint in his eye. Andrew was friendly and easy to get to know but there was always a sense of danger about him. His friend Alan was even friendlier, probably due to his liking for brandy. Alan could swear like a trooper in English, his favourite word being 'cunt'. He would often enter the casino and address me as the 'Red cunt'.

Another of the regular Chinese punters was a guy called Tommy a.k.a Buncan. He would come in with the other guys but he was more independent and would often come in alone. He was a lot older than the others, or at least he looked it. He was fat and wrinkly with false teeth, he would get them out at any opportunity. Tommy was crazy in an amusing and dangerous way but he was always good for a laugh and never got angry when he did his brains.

One of our regular night time punters was a Dutch guy called Jan. He was a champion kick boxer, mean looking and very violent. I liked him. One night he was sat at the bar on his own having a quiet drink when suddenly this guy, who was stood next to him was down on the floor and Jan slammed the sole of his foot down hard on this guys jaw with a sickening crack. He'd obviously said the wrong thing. The guy with the broken jaw was picked up and escorted off the premises. After a while Jan, having calmed down a bit also left.

Another of our regulars was a guy called Henk Bakker. He stood about six feet tall with dirty blond shoulder length receding curly hair. He had a fat face with piercing blue eyes and a foul mouth. He was a strong looking man but had gone to seed and was now all fat. He was a major high roller who would often pack a semi-automatic in a shoulder holster and he hated losing. Henk would shower me with abuse in Dutch, which at the time I didn't understand. One of his favourites was to call me a 'Kanker English' which I later found out from Hank roughly translated as wishing cancer on me.

On a lighter note, another of our regular night time visitors was this very cute Thai girl called Pan. She had a very seductive voice, long black shiny hair, a beautiful face and a perfectly slim sexy body. Pan liked to wear some very revealing clothes. Her jeans were always very tight showing of her pert round bottom. She would always come in and flirt with me and would often sit at the bar looking at me with her legs wide open in her tight jeans. Use your imagination. I fancied her something rotten and I thought I was in there until Hank pointed out to me that she used to be a man and she'd had a sex change. That dampened my desire I must say, but I'd still meet up with her for a drink and a joint occasionally. It turned out she lived across the road from the Village Hotel with her husband. The Louis Seize attracted a lot of serious high rolling punters and Terry and I were in our element.

At the beginning of our second week at the hotel we went to see Rudy to pay another weeks rent. It was then that he turned round and asked us if we were croupiers working in the city. We didn't know what to say. He could see we were working out what to say to him when he told us not to worry. He knew a lot of the croupiers in town. It turned out that many of the croupiers frequented the nightclub below the hotel. Working continuous nights we hadn't had the pleasure of visiting it yet. It was called the Homolulu.

Whilst Terry went out to get something to eat I stayed at the bar with Rudy and we got chatting. He was a round fat jolly man with thick black curly hair and dark eyes. I liked him straight away, he was a good host. He asked me if we were looking for a flat. I told him we were and he immediately offered me a one bedroom flat round the corner. I told him I was interested so Rudy got one of his assistants Istvan, to take me to the flat.

The flat was on the Korte Leidsedwarsstraat. One canal down and closer to the Leidse Plein. The ground floor was a bar. The vacant flat was on the next floor and it just so happened that Istvan and Mike, Rudy's two assistants lived in the top flat. It was Rudy's building, no wonder he knew of a flat going.

I was shown into the flat. The door opened into a small living space. A few steps in and there was a door on my right. This opened into a long rectangular fully tiled shower room with a toilet. Round the corner from the bathroom was more floor space with a kitchen along one wall. The place was well decorated and the floor was tiled. Large windows took up one side of the flat looking out onto the street below with a little balcony. Climbing the spiral staircase I was already to say yes to the flat. Seeing the bedroom made me certain I was going to take it.

The bedroom was as big as the downstairs floor space. It was split levelled with mirrored wardrobes on two walls. Then I noticed the bed. It was sunk into the floor. The bedroom was like something out of a porn movie. I decided to take the flat. We went back to the hotel. I was ecstatic, I had a job, I had money in my pocket and now I had a luxurious flat close to the Leidse Plein and a short walk to work. Rudy wanted one months rent of six hundred guilders up front and that was it. He handed me the keys and I went to find Terry.

I told Terry I'd got myself a flat. I explained it was only a one bedroom flat but he could crash on the settee until he found his own place. On seeing the flat he readily agreed. We were out of the hotel and into our own living space. Things were just getting better and better.

CHAPTER SIX
I WANT TO BUY SOME COCAINE

Terry and I had been working for a solid two weeks at the Louis Seize. Our pockets were full of cash and we were looking forward to our first days off. A few days earlier we had moved into my new flat just off the Leidse Plein. Two items were essential for our first days off. A gram of cocaine and a bag of Afghan hash. The hash wasn't a problem, there are coffee shops all over Amsterdam. The trouble was the cocaine. I hadn't had the chance to make an acquaintance with any cocaine dealers.

I decided to ask Hank if he knew any coke dealers. "Hank," I said "I've got two days off coming up, a new flat and a pocket full of cash where can I get some coke?" He thought awhile then said "Ask the boss."

"Ask the boss, are you mad, he'll fire me?" I thought Hank was on a wind up.

"No he won't, go and ask him you'll be fine." He said.

So I did. I went into the office as bold as brass. Erwin was sat behind his desk. "Erwin can I ask you a question?" I inquired.

"Of course you can, come on in." He said.

I closed the door and approached Erwin at his desk a little apprehensively. I gave him the same story I'd given Hank. "I've got two days off, a new flat and a week's wages in my pocket where can I get some cocaine?" Erwin thought awhile then replied "Leave it with me I'll see what I can find for you, come and see me tomorrow." That was that. I left the office and went back to work.

The next day I went and found Erwin in the office and asked him if he'd been able to find some coke for me. "I asked around for you Red and the people I spoke too only deal in kilos." I was taken back a bit. I only wanted a gram.

"How much is a kilo?" I asked in my naivety.

"About twenty five thousand guilders." Erwin replied.

"Shit I can't afford that I was only looking for a gram." I said.

Erwin reached into the top pocket of his jacket and pulled out a small sealed plastic bag. Throwing it across his desk at me he said "Here, that's for you, a little sample, have good days off."

"How much do I owe you?" I asked.

"Nothing it's free."

"Oh, O.K., thanks." I said, and left the office.

What Erwin had given me turned out to be a gram of almost pure cocaine which Terry and I thoroughly enjoyed on our days off. I later learnt from Hank that my bosses happened to be the biggest coke dealers in town. As I never managed to raise twenty five thousand guilders I never asked Erwin for any more cocaine.

CHAPTER SEVEN
DAYS OFF

Monday. Terry and I were working the day shift before our days off. This would be our first days off and we were looking forward to being let loose on the city. Before coming over to Amsterdam I had been asked to pass a message to a guy called Frank from a friend of mine in London. Frank used to be a casino manager at the Colony Club in London.

Previously I'd asked Hank if he knew the guy and where I would find him. Hank told me he knew him and that he occasionally came into the casino. Later that afternoon Frank walked into the casino and Hank pointed him out to me. I introduced myself and passed the message on to him and went back to dealing blackjack. Just before he left Frank came over, thanked me and shook my hand leaving two one hundred guilder notes carefully folded in the palm of my hand.

Amsterdam was just getting better and better. Everyday I was learning something new. That day I was working with an Indian girl called Cheryl. She had long thick curly hair, dark eyes and a mole on her left cheek. She was beautiful to look at and beautiful to know. Cheryl also had these very long perfectly manicured finger nails which I was amazed she could deal with. But she managed quite well.

She explained to me that the Louis Seize was also known as the '88'. Most of the casinos in the city didn't have names so they were just known for their building number like the '217' the '66' or the number

5. Casinos I would later get to know and work in. At ten o'clock Liz, Veronica and Chrissie came in. Terry and I picked up our wages and along with Hank we went out for a few drinks.

We met up with Paul and Eve and Hank took us to this posh nightclub near the Leidse Plein called the Blanc de Blanc. It was an expensive place but our pockets were bulging with cash. We were all enjoying the music and the ambiance, chatting away and just chilling out. Any new club or bar was a whole new experience for Terry and me so we were loving it.

A couple of pretty ladies came over to join us. Hank and Paul knew them. A fresh round of drinks arrived and we all got comfortable. Terry, the ladies man, steamed into one of them and I got talking to the other one. Her name was Trixie. She was pretty and fit and we were both getting along nicely, chatting away, laughing and joking.

After a while Trixie and her friend got up and went to the ladies. Hank came and sat next to me and whispered in my ear that I was busy chatting up Frank's girl friend. I wasn't going to fuck with Frank so I knew this wasn't going anywhere but we continued on through the night and a good time was had by all.

The next day was Tuesday, Dave and Paul's day off. We were in the city with Hank, he was showing us around. Terry made a phone call too see what Dave was up to that night. We found out that Paul was out with Eve and Dave was off to the Blanc de Blanc again later that night. We spent the day wandering around the city with Hank and after grabbing a bite to eat we went back to the flat to clean up and slip into our going out gear and smoke a joint. Hank didn't hang around he went straight to the Blanc de Blanc.

When we arrived at the Blanc de Blanc Hank was sat at the end of the bar nursing a drink. We joined Hank and ordered some beers. After a while Dave and Cathy turned up. Dave got chatting to Hank, I chatted to Cathy and Terry got chatting to everybody else. Chrissie arrived with a girl called Tula and sat down with us. By now the atmosphere was buzzing.

The night quickly went by and we were the last ones left in the bar. We would have continued if it wasn't for the police coming in and telling the owner it was time to close. Dave and Cathy went off to eat, Chrissie decided to go home. Terry and Tula took Chrissie to get a taxi and Hank and I nipped into the flat and smoked half a joint then trundled off to the Homolulu.

When we arrived Terry was busy wandering around the bar socialising. I got a round of drinks in and sat down chatting with Tula. I rolled a mild Lebanese hash joint. Terry kept coming over and the atmosphere kept exploding. Someone had given him a line of cocaine. Time ticked by and at three forty five Tula requested a grass joint so I rolled one for her.

Clark and his brother Colin turned up with Jackie in tow. They joined us and our peace was shattered. Clark and Colin didn't hang around for long and they split to god knows where. Jackie remained and the four of us got wasted. At about five a.m. it was time to go. I walked Tula to the taxi rank then went home to crash.

The next day, nursing a severe hangover and generally feeling sorry for myself Paul came round to the flat to pick me up. Terry had gone out somewhere. I freshened up and feeling hungry Paul took me to an Indian restaurant about five doors down from me. I'd been too busy working and partying to notice it before.

It was your typical Indian restaurant. Long and narrow with the usual Indian decorations and music playing in the background. Along the wall were these comfortable looking booths and Paul and I settled ourselves into one of them. I was scanning the menu but Paul insisted I try a 'Thali'. I'd never heard of it before so I gave it a go. A Thali consisted of eight to ten Indian dishes in small round pots set on a round tray with a bigger pot of rice in the middle accompanied with nan bread and a raita. It was a thoroughly enjoyable and new experience. Afterwards I was introduced to the delights of being given a steaming hot damp flannel which Paul explained was to be put on my face as a refreshing aftermath to a hot curry. I was hooked and I became a regular at the restaurant often to be seen enjoying a Thali.

The following night I was introduced to another culinary experience. About a dozen of us went to this Indonesian restaurant on the Rembrandts Plein. We ordered a 'Rice table' for all of us. After a Thali I was intrigued what was about to come next. We weren't disappointed. Slowly our table filled up with dishes of different meats, fish, vegetables, salads and nuts. They just kept coming. In the middle of the table surrounded by all these wonderful looking mixed dishes a large pot of rice was placed.

Paul explained that the way to enjoy this delicacy was to take a small portion of rice then select something from one of the dishes and enjoy the different tastes. But being English and ignorant we just piled our plates with rice and a mixture of dishes as we would have done back in England. With plenty of cold beers to wash it all down the meal was enjoyed by all. After we'd finished gorging ourselves we settled back to coffee and brandy's and I rolled a joint. I was nearly finished when one of the waiters came over. I thought he was going to tell me I couldn't smoke it in the restaurant. Instead he had a box of matches with him. I slipped the roach in the end and he kindly lit the joint for me. This was too good to be true. As a cloud of hash smoke hung over our table we ordered more drinks, sat back, relaxed and got stoned and drunk.

CHAPTER EIGHT
AUGUST 1981

Working the night shift with Liz was very profitable. When the casino was quiet we'd play backgammon for ten guilders a point. I won quite a lot. It became routine for Liz to ask for her wages half way through the shift so she could pay me off. She wouldn't quit though, just kept on playing.

Terry and I were enjoying ourselves. We were doing a lot of dope and acid and the occasional line of cocaine. We were beginning to find out the best clubs to go to for picking up cocaine. We were out there visiting bars and nightclubs and checking out the other illegal casinos in town and getting to meet all the other English croupiers.

One of the casinos we came across was the '217' on the Spuistraat just round the corner from Dam Plein which was run by a guy called Jimmy Tong. Jimmy was a happy smiling Indonesian with tight curly black hair and dark shining mischievous eyes. Jimmy had quite a crew working for him. One of them was Indonesian Michael. Short black hair, dark skinned and skinny. I found out that Michael was Liz's boyfriend. The '217' at the time was a typical casino. No windows and low lighting. It was a big place which housed a couple of American roulette tables and about three blackjack tables. There was a bar down one end and dotted around the room and along one wall were numerous card tables always busy with countless nationalities playing mainly Kalooki.

On one of our wanderings around town we came across a couple of croupiers called Kim and Dominic, they were working at one of the other casinos. We were strolling through the Leidse Plein when this guy approached us and asked us for a job. His name was Tommy. He was taller than me with a shock of curly brown hair, skinny, like me, and he was from up Liverpool way. He was a casino manager back home. It just so happened that we were looking for more staff at the Louis Seize so I took him to the casino, he did a table test and he got a job.

Terry and I went to work that night. Another quiet shift. I was playing backgammon with Liz and winning. Terry was learning how to play Russian poker from Harry. Liz had just handed me one hundred and fifty guilders when this guy came in.

He shook Theo's hand and they had a quick chat. After a while he came over and showed us a collection of watches he was selling. They were all fakes, but good looking fakes. I ended up buying a really nice Cartier and a chunky Rolex for only one hundred and fifty guilders.

We finished our shift and Ann, one of the girls we were working with wanted to go for a gamble. We'd heard about this casino in the Rembrandts Plein so we thought we'd go and check it out. We couldn't find it so we trekked off to the good old Cabala.

Terry and Ann wasted no time and got down to gambling whilst I got the drinks in. Ann steamed in fast, lost and went home at about eight o'clock. Terry and I got into the whisky and beers. I lost about one hundred guilders, Terry lost a little bit more. Down with the money, down with the whisky, at ten o'clock we decided to split.

Terry was off his trolley, so was I, but not so bad. We fell out of the Cabala into a busy and bright city morning. I'd worked out the quickest route home avoiding the morning crowds but Terry wanted to play. Terry suggested we take a stroll down the Kalverstraat. He wanted to go into the American bookshop. So we did. He wandered round the ground floor without looking at or picking up a book then went straight out the door again. He did the same with the clothes shop and the record shop. Eventually after steering him away from the Hot Potato cafe I got him home at about eleven o'clock and we crashed.

The next night at work I met a French girl called Chantelle. She was about five feet tall and the same wide. Her speciality was shop lifting. She would shop lift to order but only dealt in woman's clothes. She only stole quality gear. She was that good that she brought in brochures for the girls to look at and place an order. Size, colour, and style, whatever you wanted. A few days later she would reappear and complete her business.

I also met a guy called Alex. He too was only five feet tall with a shiny shaven head. He was from Indonesia. He sold lottery tickets. Only these tickets weren't strictly legal. It was an illegal lottery based on the legal lottery draws held every Saturday. He explained to me how it worked and I bought a ticket.

I was working more day shifts than night shifts. I preferred it this way, the day shifts were busy and more consistent than the night shifts. We could be working non stop from the time we opened until change over at ten p.m. Terry had taught Tommy and me the game of

Russian poker. Each player got thirteen cards and we had to make up two poker hands of five cards and lay the remaining three cards at the top to make a third hand. It was a good game and we played it as often as we could. We even played it when we were out in the bars. We usually played for five guilders a point. Some times serious money would change hands.

Tommy was on the same shift as Terry, Liz and me. When things were quiet we would all play each other at backgammon. Liz was still losing a lot. When we weren't playing backgammon Tommy, Terry and I would be sat at the poker table with Harry playing Russian poker.

Early one evening I was playing backgammon with Tommy on the blackjack table. The doorbell rang and Harry went down the stairs to open the door. He came back up first and walked through the door way. Tommy and I looked up to see who it was. If it was a punter we'd have to go back to work.

What we saw was a vision of beauty. Standing in the door way with her arms up and her hands resting on the door frame wearing a fur coat was a female. She had long blond hair, big blue eyes, a cheeky smile and a fine looking chest. She was a croupier, she was looking for a job and her name was Kirsten. Tommy and I caught Theo's eye as he moved in on her like the lecherous bugger he was. We gave him a nod as if to say 'give her a job.' He nodded back as if to say 'don't worry I will.' Kirsten did a table test and passed with flying colours. Theo brought her over and introduced her to everyone. She started work the next day.

A few days later two more croupiers turned up looking for work. They were a couple of scousers, Pauline and Jean. Pauline had long curly brown hair, big brown eyes and was also a good looker and Jean was blond, short, skinny, blue eyed and had a bad habit of biting her nails down to the bone. They passed their table test and joined our ever growing crew of English croupiers.

Pauline and Jean moved into a flat on the Bosboom Toussaintstraat. It was a strange place. I think maybe at one time it might have been a night club. It was on the ground floor. You'd walk through the front door then down a long dark corridor before emerging into their living room with a kitchen at the back. Being a couple of party animals we spent a lot of time at the girls flat smoking and drinking and having a good time.

Hank enjoyed spending his time with us crazy English so he was always at Pauline and Jean's as well. Hank had an English girl friend also called Pauline. She owned a Red Setter dog, drove a Mini and was always jealous of Hank hanging around with other women. One night she went a bit over the top and came round the flat on Bosboom Toussaintstraat and started banging on the door demanding entry. When we ignored her she climbed back into her Mini and drove it through the front door. She got our attention and Hank left with her to calm her down.

CHAPTER NINE
AND LIFE GOES ON
(WRITINGS FROM 1981)

I suppose you can't get more bohemian. Sat on the bedroom balcony with a grass joint, a cold beer, a line of cocaine fresh up the nose, the sun shining and 'Sandinista' by The Clash playing loud to my left.

Rolled out of bed at one thirty p.m. Washed and dressed putting on my tight straight legged unwashed faded blue jeans, yesterday's socks and my old blue canvas rubber soled shoes. On top I slipped my new khaki T shirt. With my imitation Cartier watch around my wrist and my Gauloise cigarettes firmly in my back pocket I went out and did my usual shopping run around the corner.

I bought my usual supplies of milk, orange juice, apples, bananas, nuts and cheese and went back to the flat. After putting away my shopping I decided to roll a hash and grass joint and indulge in a line of coke. I put some reggae on the stereo and went upstairs to sit on my bedroom balcony to smoke my joint and catch a bit of sun on my arms.

That wasn't to last long as I had washing to do. I finished the joint, packed my dirty washing while I listened to 'Cocaine' by J.J. Cale then slipped out to the launderette on Bosboom Toussaintstraat. I dropped off my usual four kilogram, eight guilder bag of dirty clothes and headed back to the Leidse Plein to the newsagents.

I bought the new edition of Time magazine, a Tom Robbins book and the Daily Mail. Back at the flat I went back to sitting on the balcony. With the sun at my window I had no need to go out. I stripped off my T shirt and sat on the bedroom balcony reading the Daily Mail and sipping on a cold beer.

I finished reading the paper and flicked through Time magazine. My beer was warm and flat so I went downstairs, rolled another joint, snorted a healthy line of cocaine and cracked a fresh can of beer. I took the cassette player upstairs, put 'Sandinista' back on the stereo and commenced to write sat out in the hot sun.

Typical day off. Set the alarm for midday and got up at three fifteen p.m. I picked up my dirty washing and went to the launderette across the canal. I dropped my clothes off and went for a cup of tea at the coffee shop and read some MAD magazines. I returned home at about four forty-five with my clean washing, picking up some essentials from the mini market on the way.

When I got home I rolled a joint, made a coffee and found out I'd won fifty guilders on the illegal lottery. I made my bed putting on my red and white striped sheets and put away my clean clothes. I decided to paint the walls of my bedroom but I had a headache so I had something to eat instead, cold chilli con carne from a tin.

After a while I felt better so I changed into my painting clothes and finished putting an undercoat on the walls. My headache returned so I finished up, smoked a joint, drank a glass of orange juice then had a shower. I'd been trying to ring Cathy all day but wasn't getting a reply, I needed to pick up Paul's suitcases. I wrote a letter to my mother, watched some TV, got stoned and went to sleep. Regaining consciousness at midnight I spoke to Paul on the telephone.

One Saturday in September 1981 I got out of bed at four thirty p.m. Had a shower and had something to eat. I went out to pick up a painting and do some shopping. Back at home I snorted two lines of impure cocaine. Made a coffee, smoked a joint and ate a bag of psilocybin mushrooms. And so the day begins. Still my bohemian self, dressed in a jumper and corduroys and tripped out in Amsterdam listening to Bob Dylan on the cassette player.

Note from Terry September 1981.

'Tuesday, sometime September 1981 something or other. Preparations are underway for a jaunt to the Melkweg, a together head is essential for such ventures. I shall attempt to score a woman as a welsh rarebit has left me with an appetite for more than a fifty guilder sausage session. Mark is busy blunting a razor blade on the TV. Hope I get to declare the cunt hunt open. When you read this the night would have been and gone and I hope this note will jog your memory so you can tell me what went on.'

On the sixteenth of October 1981 I was strolling around the Leidse Plein when I noticed these small posters on the lamp posts. They were advertising The Grateful Dead at the Melkweg. I gave a double take. For such a big band the advertising was small. I thought it was a wind up. But there it was, The Grateful Dead playing two nights at the Melkweg, the sixteenth and the seventeenth. The sixteenth was the last of my two days off.

I went round the corner to the Melkweg and got it confirmed. I bought a ticket for that night's concert. Wasn't going to miss this for the world. One of my favourite bands and I was going to get to see them twice in one year. The last time was at the Rainbow Theatre in London on the twenty first of February.

That night I got well and truly stoned and joined all the other Dead Heads down at the Melkweg for one unforgettable evening. They played for about three hours and eventually the gig had to come to an end. I left the Melkweg feeling elated at having seen The Dead in Amsterdam but disappointed that I'd miss the next evening as I had to go back to work.

CHAPTER TEN
DEAD OLD LADIES

The summer of 1981 was a long hot exciting one. There was always something going on and new things to experience and explore. Tommy called round the flat one afternoon and suggested we go out for a drink. We walked down the road towards the Leidse Plein. All the bars had their doors and windows open with tables and chairs set up outside. We walked into a bar we'd never been in before just to check it out. At the bar we ordered a couple of beers and noticed there was an empty pool table in the back.

We racked the balls and started to shoot some pool. Looking around us we noticed that the bar, though not busy, was full of men. Then it dawned on us, we'd walked into a gay bar. This didn't bother us. We weren't bothering them, they weren't bothering us. Maybe they thought Tommy and I were a couple, who knows, we certainly didn't care. We were getting used to the care free attitude of the Amsterdammers.

We were enjoying several relaxed games of pool and knocking back several cold beers when Kim and Kirsten joined us. It being summer the girls looked fantastic. Kirstin with her long shiny blond hair, blue eyes and big tits and Kim with her long brunette hair, brown eyes and big tits. Both of them wearing skin tight jeans was enough to turn any mans head. They certainly turned mine and Tommy's if not anyone else in the bar. The quiet atmosphere of the bar was shattered by the arrival of these two temptresses. With the pair of them leaning and sprawling over the pool table flashing their tits and asses I think the bar tender used the excuse of me just about to spark up a joint to ask us to drink up, pay up and leave. We weren't going to argue, we just went onto the next bar.

Back at work I was now working the day shift. Which suited me as it was a whole lot busier than the night shift. I preferred to work continuous for eight hours rather than sit around and end up working frantically for two hours. It also gave me the nights free to go out and party, which was every night. As I was becoming a regular in several of the bars round the city I was usually greeted with 'hello Red, your usual?' which was great if I happened to walk into a bar that was busy. Within minutes of me sitting down at the bar, a double scotch, no ice, and a beer were placed in front of me.

I always ordered a double because I was used to English measures which were pathetic. One sniff and they're gone. I got used to knocking a double scotch back in one and ordering another. It wasn't until years later I realised that a single measure on the continent was the equivalent of an English double. So I'd been knocking back quadruples all that time.

I used to get so pissed on scotch and beer I would stagger home on auto pilot. I got into the habit of knowing when I'd had enough, usually two doubles before falling unconscious. I wouldn't say goodnight, I'd just get up and go. I'd wake up in the morning in bed, with little recollection of the night before. Which used to piss my girlfriends of as I'd be there one minute and gone the next.

Waking up in the mornings I would be ravenous so before work I would go out for breakfast. Breakfast for me wasn't your usual cereal or toast. If it wasn't a Dutch breakfast of ham, eggs and cheese on bread it was usually pasta or a pizza, Sometimes a quick trip to MacDonald's or Burger King. If my stomach was up to it I might even venture a curry. Or I'd visit one of two Mexican restaurants in town. If I felt like treating myself I'd go to one of the many Argentinean restaurants that were dotted around the city and enjoy a succulent steak. Refuelled on fine food and feeling human again I'd then go and do another eight hours in the casino.

Dealing a quiet game of blackjack one afternoon I found out just how versatile Italian Tony was. This Tunisian poker dealer came in to see him and they stood in the middle of the floor in front of me having a conversation. Big deal, so what, only they spoke to each other in five different languages. Dutch, German, English, French and Italian. It was amazing to watch and listen to especially as they would change language in the middle of a sentence.

Every day at the '88' we used to have this sweet little old lady come in and play blackjack. For the life of me I can't remember her name so I'll call her Betty. She must have been in her late seventies, early eighties. She'd come in play blackjack all day, never any trouble or a bad word said.

What happened this one particular day I was not witness to. The details were later told to me down at the bar after work. I'd been dealing blackjack to Betty for most of the day and as late afternoon approached it was time for her to leave. Betty cashed in her few remaining chips, said goodbye and went to leave the casino.

Now to exit the casino you had to descend the stairs. The stairs in the '88' were for Amsterdam very wide but for Amsterdam were typically steep. From what I was told as Betty made her way down the stairs she had a heart attack and the subsequent tumble caused her to depart this earth.

Being an illegal casino or 'kok huis', in Dutch, we couldn't exactly involve the law, especially with a dead body on the premises. So Theo and Hank tidied Betty up and between them they 'walked' her the forty meters or so down the road to Rembrandts Plein and 'sat' her down in the back of one of the trams with her handbag on her lap and left her to it, so to speak.

Nothing further was heard of the incident so we assumed that the authorities found Betty and put it down to a little old lady suffering a heart attack whilst riding on a tram.

CHAPTER ELEVEN
HOW COME WE NEVER GET RAIDED?

Summer gently slipped into autumn. It was about mid October. The tourists were going home and it was that time of the year when the Amsterdam police raided the casinos. During the summer they left us to it. Everybody was making money and they had thousands of tourists to watch over. With the city slowing down they had to show the authorities in power that they were on top of the illegal gambling activities in the city.

The police usually raided the casinos anytime from early evening to the early hours of the morning. Nobody was safe we could get hit at any time with no warning. Two to three casinos would be raided and closed down in the space of a week. We at the '88' were getting a bit jittery as more casinos were being closed. It was only a matter of time before we would receive a visit ourselves.

As time went by it seemed as if we were going to be lucky as we didn't attract the attentions of the police. I asked Leo, how come we never got raided. He explained that the police left us alone for a reason. He told me if the police closed us down we would take our activities deeper underground. As we attracted some major players in town, in more ways than one, the police would leave us open for business, so if they needed to pick up any 'undesirables' they knew where to find them. I was glad we attracted some major 'undesirables' to the casino. I got to stay in work.

Our immunity didn't last. It was Thursday the 22nd of October. It was my day off. Terry was at work on the day shift. I dropped a tab of acid at about nine o'clock, lit up a joint and sat down to do a jigsaw puzzle on the table. At about ten thirty I was quietly tripping away when Terry returned home and told me we'd been raided. He told me the police had been trying to get in all day. Eventually at the change of shift at ten o'clock they gained entry.

Terry was sat between the tables and the police told him to move. Getting up from his seat he asked Erwin on the sly if he could go. Erwin said yes so Terry picked up his coat and just walked out of there. He went to play some slot machines in an arcade down the road.

Meanwhile back at the '88' all hell broke loose. Several people were arrested and carted off to jail in handcuffs. Others had their names and addresses taken and were released. All the tables were taken apart and along with all the equipment were taken away in vans. The hard liquor behind the bar was also confiscated.

When Terry returned from the amusement arcade the street was full of punters and staff and others from the local bars and restaurants milling around, asking questions and spreading rumours. Then Terry came home and got me. There was a bit of a tradition in Amsterdam amongst the croupiers. When a casino got raided all the croupiers who were free and not working had a party. We'd all congregate in a bar or nightclub and get drunk. When those members of staff who had been nicked were freed they always somehow found out where we were and we'd all continue drinking, celebrating their freedom.

The next day Terry and I were terribly hung over. We got up and went back to work as if nothing had happened. We buzzed the door and were let in. Several of the staff were there along with Theo, Erwin and Leo. The casino was bare without its tables. Supplies were being delivered, booze, food and soft drinks. It was obvious we were going to be re-opening. I asked Erwin where we were going to get more equipment from. He told me and Terry to follow him. We left the casino and climbed into a big white van and off we went.

We asked Erwin where were we going but he just said wait and see. We didn't drive far. We ended up in the Red Light district down one of many narrow side streets. We got out of the van and walked into this large non-descript warehouse. Inside was a treasure trove of gambling equipment. Roulette tables, roulette wheels, blackjack tables, baccarat tables and poker tables. There were stacks of playing chips all neatly boxed up, roulette balls, blackjack shoes and boxes of brand new playing cards. There were stacks of stools and chairs and boxes of lighting equipment, just about everything we needed to re-equip the '88' and get back to business.

While Erwin checked out the tables and the wheels, Terry and I gathered together all the chips and cards and balls and shoes that we would need. With everything stacked up in the middle of the warehouse Erwin did some wheeling and dealing and passed over a wad of cash. I asked Erwin where all this equipment came from. He told me it all came from the casinos that had recently been raided. Work that one out. So we loaded up the van and drove back to the casino and unloaded.

More staff had arrived and we all mucked in and within a couple of hours we were open for business.

CHAPTER TWELVE
THE PALESTINIAN PUNTER

Early November. Since re-opening we hadn't had any further trouble from the law and business was good. I was working the night shift. It had been a busy night but it was beginning to wind down with only a few punters remaining. We had this one guy in who I'd never seen before. He was playing American roulette and dropping a lot of dollars across the table. He must have been in for about fifteen thousand dollars and we knew he had a lot more in his wallet.

Tommy and I were at the bar taking a break when Leo came over. Leo was Jewish, the guy at the table was a Palestinian. No love lost there then. Leo gave us instructions on what he wanted us to do. "We'll stay open until we've cleaned this guy out. I want you to pay him out using short stacks."

"I'm not sure I can do that Leo, it goes against my training." I told him.

"No problem Leo, I'll deal, Red, you can chip for me and make the stacks nineteen." Said Tommy.

"Ok let's go." I said and we went back to the table.

Tommy was an ex casino manager from England and knew his stuff. While I chipped up in stacks of nineteen instead of twenty Tommy paid out all bets shaving the odds by one, thirty four instead of thirty five, sixteen instead of seventeen etc. Our Palestinian friend had no idea as we plied him with double whisky's on the house and started to slowly empty his wallet. Four o'clock, our usual closing time, came and went. Members of staff surplus to requirements were paid and sent home. Tommy and I were in full flow as the dollars kept coming.

Two hours and fifty thousand dollars later our Palestinian friend was cleaned out and left the premises. Leo was a happy man. He paid all the staff that had stayed on four hundred guilders. Double our usual wage of two hundred for an extra two hours work. Not a bad day's work.

CHAPTER THIRTEEN
FIRE IN THE '88'

Terry had been doing too much acid, dope and booze. He wasn't going round the bend. He wasn't going mad. He was still perfectly sane and could still do his job but, he'd found religion. He was beginning to get on everybody's nerves especially mine.

He started to give his money and clothes away to the beggars on the streets. He took to carrying at least three bibles and he would read them all day long. He would come home from work or wherever he'd been that day and start quoting passages to me. I knew my bible and I really didn't need this every day. He would even turn up at work with no shoes on. Theo took to calling him Jesus. He would say "Hey Red, take Jesus off that roulette table he's beginning to piss off the punters."

As my birthday was approaching on the eleventh of November I decided I wanted a bit of space so I told Terry to make himself scarce for a week as he was beginning to get on my nerves. He didn't make a fuss. He packed a bag and left me to it. I later learned that he'd moved in with Virginia who had a flat on the Damstraat, on the edge of the Red Light district. Poor old Virginia she had a heart of gold.

My birthday came and went. Just another excuse to get drunk and stoned. When I told Terry to come home he turned up with this American guy called Stefan. Stefan was wearing a long overcoat and when I suggested we go out for a drink he pulled out a long set of bolt cutters. I asked him what he was doing carrying them around with him.

He explained that he was a student in Amsterdam and he had to supplement his student grant by nicking and selling bicycles. Stefan hung out with us until the time came for him to return to the States.

We continued working and partying and I continued to explore the city. Terry and I were back on day shifts. It was early December. We turned up for work at our usual time of one thirty for opening at two. We wouldn't be working the tables this day as the night before the '88' had suffered a fire. It wasn't too serious, a fuse had been responsible behind the bar, which was the only part of the casino to be gutted. The rest of the casino was unworkable due to smoke damage.

Terry and I were instructed to go inside and start dismantling the tables. Meanwhile Theo and Erwin went off to find other premises we could use while the casino was redecorated. Terry and I entered the blackened smoke smelling casino and started to gather together the tools of our trade. The roulette wheels were moved out to the top of the stairs. The roulette balls were collected. The cards gathered. Table chips bagged. The blackjack floats were brought out of the office and placed at the top of the stairs with all the other equipment we could salvage.

We then turned our attention to the tables. We soon found out there was nothing we could do as we didn't have any tools to unbolt the tables. We didn't know when the boss was going to return so there was only one thing we could do. We upturned three empty Heineken crates and got the backgammon board out.

That's where we were found an hour later by Theo. Sat in a blackened casino playing backgammon and drinking warm Heineken beer. Tools were produced and the tables were dismantled. We took everything down the stairs onto the street and hurriedly put it in the back of a recently rented van, keeping a look out for any passing police patrols. The casino was locked up and Terry and I climbed into the van with Big Jan the driver.

Big Jan lived up to his name. He carried a big fat wobbly belly. His bald head was also big and fat and shaped like a giant pill and he had dangerously looking big hands. He wasn't the smartest of the bunch but he was a lovable guy and I would often pop round to his houseboat for a beer and he would proudly show me his Jacuzzi, always promising to get a couple of girls in for us both to enjoy.

We didn't know where we were going but it was to be a short drive. About ten minutes later we pulled up outside a building on the Geldersekade along side a canal near a building called 'The Weeping Tower' close to the railway station. Big Jan opened the door to the van without looking and knocked a cyclist off his bike. Big Jan made his apologies and we unloaded the van taking all the equipment inside.

The new premises was a large ground floor room with a kitchen and toilets leading off from it. Inside an army of helpers had arrived. Members of staff were on hand to put the tables together. New table layouts arrived and were fitted. Chips were washed, dried and stacked up on both roulette tables. The wheels were brought in, put in place and levelled. Others were laying electrical cabling and setting up the lights over the roulette and blackjack tables. Supplies of beer, spirits, soft drinks and food arrived and were put in the kitchen for Rosie to sort out.

The two toilets were labelled 'Dames' and 'Heren'. Poker tables were brought in and placed around the sides of the room with plenty of chairs. A stereo system was wired up and a TV tuned in. It was eight p.m. word went out on the streets and we were open for business at nine o'clock that night. Not a bad day's work.

Terry wasn't to be with us for much longer. By now he was really getting on everybody's nerves. He was becoming a danger to himself and was beginning to attract the attentions of the police. Having Terry in a police cell made the bosses nervous. The rest of the croupiers in town, including our lot, weren't best pleased with the idea either. He could spill the beans on everybody and everything. So it was decided the best place for him was back home in England. Paul had a word with him and got him to see sense. Everybody coughed up some money and he was put on a one way flight back to England.

Before long Christmas was upon us. It was a cold and bitter December which didn't help when one night at home my boiler decided to pack up. I had no heating and no hot water. With the flat being all glass, wood and tiles I felt like I was living inside a fridge. Until I could get Rudy to sort the problem out the next day I found it was better to wrap up warm and go out and walk the streets. The next day after an uncomfortable night trying to get some sleep I went to see Rudy at the hotel and he sent Mike back with me to get it mended.

All the casinos closed on Christmas day. Liz had a flat at the top of the Rokin near the train station. She liked to entertain and decided she was going to cook Christmas dinner for who ever wanted to come round. We all chipped in and a feast was arranged. I can't remember how many or who turned up but those that did brought a bottle of something with them. We had so many bottles of wine it was decided we would have a day of wine tasting. As you can imagine it turned into a very drunk and stoned Christmas day. For a lot of us including myself it was our first Christmas day in Amsterdam. There were to be many more.

CHAPTER FOURTEEN
FRIDAY 31st DECEMBER 1981

Another year done and on the way out. The week between Christmas and New Year was drug and alcohol fuelled. I was going the way of Terry. I was becoming irritable and short tempered. I was getting sarcastic towards my colleagues and the punters.

On New Years Eve I stayed at home. Tripped and poisoned on bad acid, high and fucked. I didn't know it was midnight until the sky outside the flat exploded with a thousand bangs, cracks and whooshes. Happy New Year, Dutch style. Nobody had told me how the Dutch celebrate New Years Eve. Looking out the window I couldn't handle all the commotion and the people down below on the street so I retired back to my sofa and the long black tunnel climbing to nowhere.

Back at work the next day people asked me where I was the night before. My reply became a favourite catch phrase 'I was gone.' We were still at The Weeping Tower, as the casino had become known. The bad trip had left me slightly unhinged and getting worse. During a break on a busy day shift I made a decision to have a holiday the following week. I spoke to Theo about this and he agreed straight off.

Arrangements were made and within days I was flying to Tangiers for a week. My plan was to travel into the Kif mountains but I had to check in mid week with my return ticket so I stayed in Tangiers. I spent a relaxing week exploring the city. Reading the Herald Tribune, soaking up the sun and working things out in my head, a sort of self analysis.

At the end of my week in Tangiers I made my way out to the airport. Due to some weird time difference between the city and the airport I missed my return flight. The next flight to Amsterdam wasn't until Wednesday but I got lucky, there was a flight leaving for London in half an hour. I bought a one way ticket, which cleaned me out. I had ten guilders left in my pocket. I would worry about that when I got to London.

My parents lived in Southend. If I could get there I could pick up some money and fly back to Amsterdam from Southend airport. I got talking to some people on the plane. They were returning home to Basildon via the A127 which would take me half way on my journey to Southend. I explained to them my situation and they agreed to give me a lift. When we arrived in London I phoned Ross, my father, and I arranged for him to pick me up at a place called Crays Hill outside Basildon. All went according to plan.

Back home Pat, my mother, fed and watered me and we went to a travel agents and Pat bought me a return ticket to Amsterdam for the next day. It was the first time I'd seen Ross and Pat since going to Holland so I regaled them with tales of Amsterdam. The next day Ross drove me to the airport and I was on my way. I flew into Schipol airport and got a train into the city. I was a day late for work so I went straight to the Weeping Tower.

I apologised to Theo for being late and told him what had happened. He remained silent so I asked him if he was going to fire me. He said he'd already fired me the day before but as I'd come straight from the station to the casino I could start work immediately. So I dropped my bag and went back to dealing roulette.

My week away had helped a little bit but I was still a bit cranky. For the next two months I came down slowly. Keeping my head together and my mouth shut. It was early March when I scored some nice cocaine. That first line of the year straightened out my head and normality was resumed. I'd become a lot thinner and paler but back then you wouldn't have noticed.

Soon after, we relocated to a place on the Herengracht behind the '88'. A luxury first floor flat across the canal from the mayor's official residence. The cheek of it don't you think? We set up business and we were there until about May. For that period as usual I just worked, got high and slept late. Not a lot happened and we didn't attract the attention of the police.

Some time in May we moved back into the '88'. We had a grand re-opening party with a buffet and plenty of bottles of chilled champagne. It was very busy that day but it felt good to be back in familiar surroundings.

CHAPTER FIFTEEN
QUEENS DAY

Winter slipped into spring. Business was good, money was being made and everybody was happy. For me everything was back to normal. We had a couple of new girls from England join us called Denise and Mirella. When the roulette was doing its brains Leo had taken to sitting at the end of the table by the wheel. If he saw the ball about to drop into a heavily bet number he would use his knees to lift the table which in turn would upset the balance of the wheel and the ball would drop into an empty number. He wasn't very subtle about it, and sometimes it was quite embarrassing.

This one particular day I was on the night shift. It had been a busy one, a profitable one and it was soon time to close. There would be no going out gambling and drinking for me as I had to be back in eight hours for a day shift. I stepped out of the casino and swung a left to head for home. When I came to the Vijzelstraat I noticed people already out and about and putting up stalls. I didn't think much of it, there was always something going on around the city.

I continued my way along the Herengracht until I got to the Leidsestraat. I swung a left and started walking down the Leidsestraat to my flat. All the way down people were putting up stalls along the road side. Now I was intrigued something major was going on. When I got to the Leidse Plein I noticed a couple of stages being erected. A sure sign of live music later in the day. I had a quick wander round then headed of home to try and get some sleep.

I got in a few hours sleep when my peace was shattered by the wailing of a guitar and the banging of drums. Someone was doing a sound check on one of the stages in the Leidse Plein. I rolled over and tried to go back to sleep. I gave up and got up. I showered, had some breakfast, got dressed and went out to investigate. I had a few hours to kill before I had to be at work.

I walked into the Leidse Plein. The square was alive with activity. There were stalls everywhere I looked. It was like a giant car boot sale. Everything and anything was being sold. It was as if all these people had emptied their attics over night and were now trying to sell everything off. There were clothes, furniture, antiques, trinkets, books, cassettes and records. You name it you could probably have bought it. Dominic even made himself a portable blackjack table with a strap to go round his neck. He wandered around offering people a game but the police soon put a stop to that.

There were people selling food and cold drinks. There were people doing barbecues and there were stalls devoted entirely to the selling of cold beer. I asked someone what was the reason for all this street madness. They told me it was Queens Day. Every year on the thirtieth of April the Queen celebrated her unofficial birthday. The same as our Queen Elizabeth did. Up and down the entire country on the streets and in the parks the citizens of Holland had one big party.

With time to kill I walked around the Leidseplein soaking up the atmosphere amazed at the amount of people out on the streets. I walked up the Leidsestraat through the masses and made my way to the Dam Plein. I fought my way through the Red Light district and down the Rokin towards the Rembrandts Plein. I bought a cheese burger and a cold beer from a stall on the Rokin and made slow progress to the casino to do my day shift. It seemed such a shame to be going to work with all this madness going on.

It was a good shift, an enjoyable one. The party atmosphere outside came into the casino. When change over came those on the day shift hit the city to party. We wandered around the city eating food, drinking beers and watching the bands play. Every where we went there was live music blasting out.

We ended up back in the Leidse Plein and finally finished up in the Homolulu until closing time then I went home to face the next morning's hangover.

CHAPTER SIXTEEN
CULTURE VULTURE

When I wasn't out getting drunk or stoned Paul introduced me to the delights of the city's cultural events. First he took me to the two great art galleries in the city. The first he took me to was a modern building, the Vincent van Gogh museum. Dedicated entirely to Vincent's paintings, drawings, etchings, watercolours and letters.

The second art gallery he took me to was the Rijksmuseum near the Leidse Plein. A vast red bricked building housing a great many works of art from paintings and drawings to statues from world famous sculptors and much more. One of many famous paintings to be found in the Rijksmuseum is the enormous painting by Rembrandt called 'The Night Watch'. The Rijksmuseum isn't the sort of building you can visit in one day so I was to return to it a great many times during my stay in Amsterdam.

Back down the vast space known as the Museum Plein next door to the Vincent van Gogh museum is the Stedelijk Museum housing many modern and contemporary works of art. Not being one for modern art this was a rarely visited art museum for me.

A short walk down the Van Baerlestraat is the Concertgebouw. Home of the Royal Concertgebouw Orchestra. Other orchestras would come and visit and being a fan of classical music I would go along anytime I wasn't working and listen to the likes of Beethoven,

Tchaikovsky, Mozart, Bach and other great composers throughout history.

Leaving the Museum Plein behind us we walked up to Dam Plein. Next to the Queens Palace stands the Nieuwe Kerk (new church). Every year in the autumn the church would house an exhibition of photography taken by photo journalists from around the world. It became an annual event to stroll around the church taking in the images captured from around the world. They always produced a book of all the photos in the exhibition.

Leaving the 'Dam' behind us we wander down The Rokin through the Munt Plein and down Reguliersbreestraat. On this street stands the Tuschinski Theatre. Dating back to the beginning of the century its design was very avant-garde. It was a beautiful building both inside and out. Primarily used as a cinema it was sometimes reverted back to a theatre. It was here many years later when my friend Gary and I enjoyed a midnight concert by Oscar Peterson.

Two of my favourite 'modern' venues in the Leidse Plein were the Melkweg (the milky way) and the Paradiso. The Melkweg was just off the Leidse Plein opposite one of the city's police stations. I think it was an old converted warehouse. It had about four floors with all sorts of stuff going on inside. Downstairs on the ground floor was the music venue area with a bar. On other floors there was a vegetarian restaurant and areas dedicated to art and other areas where you could just go and chill out and get stoned or meditate. When I first went there I asked someone where I could score some dope. They directed me to a stall on the second floor where there was a whole selection of hashish and marijuana for sale. Right next to the dope stall they had a sweet stall selling all sorts of munchies. I got to see many live bands play in the Melkweg over the years. The most memorable was seeing the Grateful Dead in 1981.

The Paradiso was also just off the Leidse Plein. It was an old converted church which was used by the old prison next door. The Paradiso was a live band venue. I would often be found there on nights off when a good band was in town. I would go on my own or with Paul and Eve, sometimes others depending who was on and what they liked. I saw some great bands there over the years too numerous to remember. When I could I would always go and see Herman Brood when he was in town. There were no seats as such to sit on, just an open floor. So I would often wander around catching the acts from different angles. Upstairs was a balcony running around three sides of the room where I would often hang out on the sides or at the back or failing that I'd just be propping up the bar.

A popular nightclub I frequented was the Homolulu on the Kerkstraat. Initially a gay nightclub catering for both homosexuals and lesbians but all were welcome. It became a regular venue for the city's croupiers, casino bosses, punters and other shady characters. Because it was a gay nightclub nobody had anything to prove so there was very little trouble inside.

It wasn't a large venue which appealed to its intimacy. There was a small restaurant at the back which did a fantastic beef stroganoff with a small second bar along side. The main bar, a big rectangular shaped thing was sat in the centre of the club so you could see all those sat at the bar, a little less intimate but great for mingling. At the other end of the club was a small dance floor often occupied by the flamboyant and outrageous. Along one wall were little booths with tables and chairs.

You would often find me enjoying a beef stroganoff in the restaurant before retiring to the bar to mingle and chat to whoever was in that night. I liked to wander round the bar chatting to different people and ordering rounds of drinks. I loved the system they had in Amsterdam, you had a tab behind the bar and paid at the end of the night. Clever really as you never knew how much you were spending. I would often go home without paying my bill but I never got any hassle over it as I would invariably be back the next night where I would settle up and start a fresh one.

Another major attraction in the city was the vast expanse of Vondel Park. Just round the corner from the Leidse Plein it was the biggest park in the city. With plenty of lakes and walkways it was the place to be, especially on Sunday's when you could find anything from clowns, magicians, jugglers and music. There was organised music from jazz to rock 'n' roll and around every corner there was always a street busker plying his or her trade. One of the concerts I caught there one day was Simply Red and Simple Minds on the same bill. Set in a natural round hollow in the park and circled by giant oak trees it was quite spectacular. It may have been raining at the time but there was a whole bunch of us there amongst a sea of colourful umbrellas with our hip flasks full and our ready rolled joints. We stayed dry and happy and a good day was had by all. There was all sorts of art going on in the park. At one time there were eleven Buddha's floating on one of the lakes. I was fortunate to get a photograph of them one day with a rainbow over their heads. Quite magical.

Venturing into Vondel Park one Queens Day was a crazy but exciting journey. The streets of the city were chaotic, the park was just as bad. The walkways were packed with people. Every bit of greenery was taken up with people selling everything imaginable. You had your usual street entertainers and live music was everywhere. The smells of burgers and hot dogs and marijuana filled the air. The city's population were in the park and out on the streets. So many people, such a big party.

CHAPTER SEVENTEEN
STEVE CRACKS HIS SQUAT

I met Steve through Kirstin. He was working as a croupier in town at the time. Around August time he 'cracked' his squat. It was on the Oudezijds Achterburgwal just the other side of the Red Light district. It was a two storey building. Old, dirty and dilapidated. You walked through the door into a downstairs room which was full of rubbish. Up the creaking stairs he had a nice size kitchen, a living room, small bathroom and toilet and a double bedroom with an uneven sloping floor. The next floor up was one large attic space with open rafters.

On my first visit Steve was busy tidying the place up. He'd done the kitchen and the living room and was working on his bedroom. He'd kitted the place out from stuff found on the streets. He took time out and we sat in the kitchen at his latest acquired table and chairs smoking a joint and drinking a cold beer from his 'new' fridge.

Steve was from Southampton. He had a shock of curly brown hair and owned a beat up old car. Steve never locked his car. He figured if he locked it the junkies would keep breaking into it. So he left the car unlocked and let the junkies use it to crash in over night. No ones going to steal a car with a junkie inside it.

One of the things about Amsterdam was that on every first Monday of the month if you had stuff you wanted to get rid of you put it out on the street. The next day it was picked up by the city refuse department. They didn't have tips like we do in England. We called it

'Monday night shopping', we'd go out and scour the streets and see what we could find.

I loved Monday night shopping. It was like one big rummage sale, only everything was free. I'd find stuff on the streets, pick it up and go round the next day to see Steve. I'd take him rugs and matting for the floor. Pots and pans and
cutlery for the kitchen, just about anything useful for setting up a home from scratch.

Before long Steve's squat was like a palace. He had wall to wall and floor to ceiling carpeting. He found himself an old cast iron double bed with extendable legs so he could have a level bed on his uneven sloping floor. He had cupboards in all rooms, a couple of wardrobes and a chest of draws in his bedroom and a matching three piece suite in his living room.

He had hot and cold running water in the bathroom and kitchen and had tapped into an electricity supply. His kitchen was fully functional with tables and chairs, a fridge and a working gas cooker. One of Steve's favourite kitchen utensil he found on the street was this large cast iron frying pan. We ended up cooking all sorts of wonderful stews and fry-ups in it. Our most common dish invariably ended up with plenty of tuna, mayonnaise and sweet corn.

The eaves in the attic space were stuffed with old single and double mattresses for insulation and he'd put boards across the roof beams to create space for storage. The ground floor room had been cleaned of rubbish, carpeted all out and a single bed installed for guests. It was soon a proper warm comfortable house.

One time I was with Steve when he was driving a friend of his to catch a ferry back home to England. We were cruising down the motorway passing all these small Dutch towns with strange names, one of which was called 'Monster'. After dropping his friend off we returned to Amsterdam. On the way back we decided to visit Monster. As Steve put it "Lets see what sort of rubbish they throw out in a place called Monster".

We turned off the motorway and entered Monster. It was late, about one thirty in the morning. We pulled up and parked and wandered round the deserted streets. It was like a ghost town. No bars, no coffee shops, no hookers, no nothing. We had one thing going for us though. It seemed that the next day was rubbish day so we started going through some black bin bags we came across. After going through several bags and not finding anything remotely interesting we gave up and drove home. Back to a place that had bars and coffee shops and hookers and plenty of everything else. Steve lived in his squat for quite a while before moving out.

CHAPTER EIGHTEEN
AND LIFE GOES ON PART TWO
(WRITINGS FROM 1982)

Quit messing about, light that joint and let's get this thing on the road. Today is or rather was Wednesday 22nd September 1982. Seven days since the appearance of Gary and Dave, two old house buddies from Stead Road in Sheffield. They came all the way from England for a week's holiday in Amsterdam.

I'd slept all day on the fifteenth last. Woke up at about five p.m. and rushed off to the launderette on Bosboom Toussaintstraat to drop off my washing. The launderette was closed and I wasn't too happy about sleeping all day. On the way back to the flat Paul passed me by on his bicycle in search of me.

Back at the flat I dumped my bags and rolled a joint. Paul reminded me I'd been invited to dinner at his place. Food was what I needed so I accepted. At eight p.m. with hot food inside me we were back at my flat on the Korte Leidsedwarsstraat getting stoned. Paul was busy running around cleaning up the place. I was wondering who was coming.

I was halfway through rolling a joint when the doorbell rang. Paul looked out the window and muttered something about the mushrooms being there. The mushrooms were in fact Gary and Dave. They'd contacted Paul about coming over without telling me. I was totally surprised, I wasn't expecting them especially tonight. "You're just in time." I said to them as they walked into the flat holding up a finished joint. With an excited exchange of conversation, bullshit and joint rolling the night began.

Three quarters of an hour later I hit the road in search of cocaine or speed to keep the boys going through the night. The first number I rang was unobtainable so I called another coke dealer I knew. He had what I needed so I scored a gram of cocaine and headed back to the flat a half hour later. The girls from work had turned up all chatting away, smoking and drinking. I chopped up the coke and passed it around to any takers. We smoked a bit more, ate some food then took Gary and Dave out to show them the city.

We toured the city showing the boys the sights and the Red Light district. We took them into The Bulldog Cafe were they bought some grass and hash. We took them to other coffee shops, to bars and some nightclubs. Come two a.m. we ended up at the Homolulu to meet up with the girls and anyone else who was out playing that night. The boys felt a bit lost and out of place in the Homolulu so we returned to the flat for some more drugs and a few moments of relaxation. They soon crashed out, it had been a long day for them.

December 24th 1982. I eventually got it together to begin my three day break, or was it four? Christmas Eve, got out of bed at three p.m. People were up and about so ACDC went into the cassette player nice and loud and rousing first thing in the morning. I had a quick wash, a glass of milk and I went out on the Leidsestraat with a half smoked afghan joint in search of a saucepan to heat my turtle soup.

I bought my saucepan, a new book and some fresh French bread and went back to the flat. With the Clash playing I ate my soup, rolled a joint and scanned the new William Burroughs book I'd bought. I washed the pots, opened a bottle of wine and continued reading with Spirit playing in the background and a gratifying warm feeling in my stomach.

Later I had a pleasant meal of oranges, Clementines, bananas, nuts and cheese washed down with a bottle of Beaujolais '82 to the sounds of Frank Zappa and the Mothers of Invention. I didn't want to see what was going on outside now. A line, a joint and another bottle of wine. Quarter past midnight, drunk, stoned and wrapped up warm. I fall asleep on the settee for a good nights sleep.

CHAPTER NINETEEN
NEW YEARS EVE 1982

I woke up about midday. I needed to get some supplies in before the shops shut. I bought some fruit, nuts, milk, bread and beers. I also picked up some new handkerchiefs for my cocaine abused nose. Back home I smoked a joint and read a bit, chilling out. I showered and put on some clean clothes ready to spend New Years Eve at Theo's house out of the city in Haarlem. He had invited his entire staff from the '88' to join him in this years festivities. Remembering last New Years Eve I wasn't going to miss this one.

At six p.m. I took a taxi round to Tommy's to join the rest of the crew. When I arrived Liz, Kirstin, Virginia, Hank and of course Tommy were already there. Denise, Mirella and Jean joined us soon after. Pauline wasn't with us, she'd already hooked up with Theo and was now living at his place. And so the day began, non stop joint rolling and plenty of alcohol. I hit the whisky when I was a little bit more awake and together, a few lines helped us on our way.

At nine thirty we decided to hit the road. Jean, Denise, Mirella and Kirstin went ahead in a taxi. Tommy, Virginia, Liz and I followed in Hank's car. At one stage we lost the girls on a bend and when we caught up there were two taxis in front of us. Which one to follow? It was dark we couldn't see what colour it was. The two taxis parted to go there separate ways, one flashed its rear lights, that's the one we thought but then the other taxi flashed his lights. We were all cracking up with laughter totally confused but then one of the taxis slowed down and we realised that was ours. We continued our way up the long straight road to Haarlem.

We arrived at Theo's and tucked into a mighty fine buffet laid on by Pauline. There wasn't much conversation at first. I think we were all a little uncertain on how to conduct ourselves at Theo's house. Having said that, a few of us were used to partying with Theo at the Homolulu. After a few drinks and joints everybody relaxed and got into the spirit of the event.

Just before midnight Theo handed me a box of fireworks and told me to go outside and at midnight let them off. Outside all of Theo's neighbours were coming out their doors also carrying boxes of fireworks. We had a count down and at midnight the church bells started ringing. I lit the fuse to a rocket and turned away as it whooshed into the sky. As I turned a guy behind me also set off a rocket right in front of me. Everybody was setting off fireworks at random all around me I had nowhere to duck. It was total chaos but exhilarating.

All our lot were hanging out the window, Theo was egging me on. People were hanging out of all the other windows up and down the street cheering and shouting and having a wonderful time. My ears were whistling like that feeling after being at a very loud rock concert.

With all the fireworks spent and the air thick with smoke and the smell of gunpowder Theo shouted down for me to catch. Catch what I thought, and then it came tumbling out of the window towards me. It was his Christmas tree. I stepped out of the way as it landed at my feet.

He told me to take the tree to the bridge and throw it on the fire. What bridge, what fire I thought, but then I noticed Christmas trees were tumbling out of windows all around me. This is bizarre I thought. I picked up the tree by its stump and followed this procession of neighbours dragging their trees to this bridge. Someone had already got a fire going and one by one trees were being added to the fire. So our tree went on as well.

Later Theo told me it was a tradition. He told me that every year they had a bonfire and every year they burnt the bridge down until recently when they'd decided to build a concrete bridge. At about two a.m. Hank, Tommy, Kirstin, Liz and I drove back to the city. Our plan was to go the Homolulu for the rest of the evening. I nipped home to change my shoes. I had a line and half a joint and went to the Homolulu.

It was crowded when I got there. The crew were already there and a whole bunch of other croupiers from the other casinos. I spent the rest of the night wandering around the bar talking, chatting and wishing everybody a happy New Year. A good night was had by all and we stayed until closing time.

CHAPTER TWENTY
LOSING MY JOB

New Years Day 1983, back to work on the night shift feeling fine. The last eighteen months in Amsterdam had hardened me to the booze and the late nights. Working in the '88' continued through the winter and into spring. News got through to us that Jan, the kick boxer had been found dead in one of the lakes outside the city. He'd been stuffed into an oil drum and his penis had been cut off and stuffed into his mouth. He'd obviously upset the wrong person.

Sometime around April an article appeared in one of the local papers revealing that Amsterdam probably had more black money in circulation than white. What with the sex, drugs and the gambling industry in the city this came as no surprise. I was a part of that black economy and I would take very little out of it. The way I saw it was, I worked, I spent, and kept my earnings in the system rather than pay taxes to the government.

April was a nice sunny month, an indicator of another nice summer to come. April turned into May and all seemed well at work, but things weren't what they seemed. Leo, Erwin and Theo had decided to have a purge on their staff. One by one they were called into the office and one by one they disappeared from our ranks. Jean was getting a bit worried so I tried to put her mind at rest telling her that we'd worked for Leo for nearly two years now, we were good workers and we'd made him some serious money.

Time came for Jean to go to the office. When she came out she looked at me and nodded her head. She was a casualty. Next it was my turn. I went into the office and Leo and Erwin were there. They thanked me for my hard work but told me they had to let me go but because of my hard work and loyalty they gave me two weeks notice to find another job. I was devastated, I thought I was invincible, I thought this could never happen to me. I didn't ask why I just accepted it.

Other casinos were also laying off staff. Many filtered out to the other cities in Holland, some crossed the border into Germany. I was comfortable and happy in Amsterdam so I decided to stay. Unfortunately there weren't any jobs going so I decided to leave the flat and go home to England for a while.

Saturday June 5th was a strange day. I was on the day shift. I got up had a shower and a cup of coffee and went round to the Village Hotel to see Rudy. I told him that I was leaving the flat but Paul and Eve were taking it over. He was happy with the arrangement, his rental income was uninterrupted. When I got back to the flat the telephone was ringing. At first I was confused wondering what it was. The telephone hadn't worked for six months. I answered it, wrong number, I tried ringing home, no reply.

I got dressed and went to work. It was a terrible day, hot, humid and to top it all we lost again. After work I went home and changed then nipped out to ring my mother. My sister Gina answered the phone, Pat and Ross were out. I told her I would be home shortly and rang off. I started to pack up my belongings. Most of my stuff I was going to leave with Paul. I intended to return as soon as there was work. I started on my collection of books upstairs in the wardrobe.

I flicked through each book one by one. I had a habit of stashing drugs and money between the pages of books. I didn't want to take any books home and get caught with drugs on me. To my surprise in one of my books I found 2500 guilders, the equivalent of £500. I was so excited at the find I rang home and got my brother Pablo. He couldn't believe that I was nonchalant about finding £500 lying around I didn't even know I had.

Paul and Eve moved in, they took the bedroom and I crashed on the settee. Paul and I had a typewriter each and we would get stoned and sit in opposite corners of the lounge and type short story's and poems, mostly utter nonsense.

I bought myself a one way ticket to England. I did my last shift for Leo, Erwin and Theo at the '88'. I finished packing my bags and on Thursday 17th June almost two years to the day I took a taxi out to Schipol airport. It was a lovely feeling leaving Amsterdam at seven fifteen a.m. The day promised to be sunny and bright. The taxi driver had Pink Floyds 'Dark Side of the Moon' playing on his cassette player. I was stoned, coked, relaxed and ready for a days travelling.

CHAPTER TWENTY ONE
MAKING A DRUG DEAL

In early July I returned to Amsterdam. I'd kept in touch with Paul and he told me there was a likelihood of work on the horizon. I still had some money left so I checked in at the Village Hotel, I even got my old room back. Pan came over to visit me with her girlfriend and we got stoned together. I remember one morning I pulled my curtains open and got back into bed and smoked a joint. Lying there getting stoned I heard this weird creaking sound. After a while I worked out it was the rubber plant in the window slowly turning to meet the morning sun. I lay there in bed and in a stoned haze actually watched this plant slowly twist and turn with the sun.

I wasn't going to be there long but while I was I had a visit from Matthew and David, a couple of old friends of mine from Sheffield. They were after buying a couple of kilos of cocaine to smuggle back to England. I knew a few small time dealers in town and the only big time dealer I knew were the guys from the '88' but as I'd recently been laid off by them I wasn't going down that route.

As I was getting a bit of a reputation as being a 'mister fix it' I told them I'd see what I could do. I hit the streets and made a few visits and a few phone calls and was soon hooked up with someone who could supply the required amount. The product on offer was cocaine paste. Cocaine in its purest form before being transformed into powdered cocaine.

I was given a price and I returned to the hotel to Matthew and Dave with the offer. They were happy with the deal so I set them up to meet the dealer. After a couple of hours they returned to the hotel having concluded business. Being a couple of experienced drug smugglers they packaged up the cocaine for smuggling back into England and the next day they returned home safely.

That was the one and only time I got involved in a big time drug deal and smuggling. As it was a favour for old friends I didn't turn any profit. A few years later they were busted after running a successful smuggling operation through France. They both got three years.

I got a job working for Jimmy Tong in the '217' on the Spuistraat. We had two American roulette tables and two blackjack tables. We were busy and it was good to be earning again. We were getting a lot of Indonesians, Surinamers and Chinese coming in and of course my good friend Henk Bakker. Jimmy was a sly bugger. Henk won ten thousand guilders one night and Jimmy counted out ten one thousand guilder notes in front of Henk and myself. Only there were eleven of them. Jimmy counted them out twice, he went one two three three four five six. It was then when I clocked it. I didn't say anything, I figured Jimmy must have had silent partners and he was on the take.

I scored some cocaine one night and the next day I was feeling really bad. When I saw Paul he said that the coke had been laced with strychnine and someone was trying to knock me off. I put that down to Paul being melodramatic. However if that were the case the person responsible would have been shocked to see me alive and well just looking a bit pale and green around the gills. If it was an attempted hit, I'd survived it.

As time went by the police stepped up their activities and several casinos had been raided. In order to stay one step ahead of the police Jimmy closed down his operation in the '217' and we moved to new premises on the corner of Weteringschans and Reguliersgracht. In the '217' we'd had this regular Chinese punter, nice man, high roller. He liked to play the second dozen to the maximum. Jimmy made sure he knew where we were in the new casino and he soon became a regular again. Pretty soon he started to have it away and was several thousand guilders ahead.

One afternoon before he came in these curtains were pulled around the roulette table. The sort of curtains you would see around a bed in hospital. I didn't know what was going on and I didn't ask. After a while the curtains were pulled back and all seemed normal. Right on cue our Chinese friend came in headed for the roulette table and was soon losing lots of money.

Now an old casino trick we use to check that the wheel hasn't been tampered with is to rest the tip of your thumb on top of the sections that sit between each number whilst the wheel is spinning. I just happened to do this and that's when I found out what had been going on behind the closed curtain. What had happened was they had slightly raised these sections which corresponded to the numbers in the second dozen. In effect what this did was, as the ball was slowing down if it hit one of these raised sections it would bounce off them and in theory land in another number, preferably not in the second dozen. The theory worked and over the course of the next few days we cleaned him out taking thousands of guilders off him. Soon after that the police caught up with us and closed us down.

I was soon back at work in the number 7 on the Nieuwezijds Kolksteeg, just off the Nieuwezijds Voorburgwal for Jimmy Tong and Tony Wu. It was an apartment above a small snack bar which was quickly adapted for our purposes. We only had two American roulette tables but business was good and I was soon back in top form.

I couldn't stay at the hotel for too long but I was fortunate that Rudy knew of a flat that I could stay in for a month before it was rented out. I was lucky, it happened to be on my old street, the Korte Leidsedwarsstraat just down from my old flat where Paul and Eve were living. It was a big flat but clearly in need of some renovation and decoration but I wasn't complaining as I had a roof over my head for at least a month.

I remember Paul coming round one afternoon and knocking me out of bed. I'd had a good night out and I was suffering a hangover from hell. This was the time before I became a hardened drinker and no longer suffered hangovers. Paul made me a strong cup of coffee and bought it into the bedroom where I was sat on the edge of the bed holding my head and groaning. He handed me the cup of coffee and I accidentally belched in his face. "That's the pits of whisky hell Red." I remember him saying.

After a month it was time to vacate that flat. I hadn't had much luck in finding a decent flat in the city centre. I'd seen a few dodgy ones on the outskirts of the city but I was fussy, I wanted something central. Fortunately my old friend Carol, who I'd worked with at the '88', offered me a place on the floor of her flat, so I took it. My place on her floor was behind the settee.

Carol shared the flat with Eric and Jerry. We all worked the night shift in different casinos. We'd all get home in the mornings and sit around smoking joints and drinking cups of tea. These guys were into their tea, cup after cup, pot after pot. They would sit for hours talking and playing loud music. In the end I would crawl behind the settee into my sleeping bag, cover my ears and try to get some sleep. After a couple of weeks of that I was glad to get out and move into more peaceful accommodation.

CHAPTER TWENTY TWO
NEW FLAT NEW JOB

From sleeping on Carol's floor I moved into a studio flat on the Reguliersgracht. Kirstin had lived here for several months now. I was often round there visiting and chilling out and visiting a girl called Debbie who lived in one of the ground floor studio flats. She just happened to be a cocaine dealer.

My flat was on the next floor up from Kirstin. It consisted of just the one room with a small kitchen along one wall, a settee, T.V. and a bed in the corner. There were two studio flats on each floor and we shared the toilet and shower. The other studio flats were quickly occupied by other English croupiers so the place, although basic, became a happy place to be. It was whilst living here that I met Kirstin's sister Justine. She wasn't anything like Kirstin. Justine had reddish hair, a round face and beautiful brown eyes. A friend of Kirstin's called Scott, from Leicester would also pop over for the occasional visit.

We were literally a couple of minutes walk from the Rembrandts Plein. The Reguliersgracht was known as the 'Seven Bridges' for obvious reasons and at night all seven bridges were lit up for the tourists. If you stood in a certain place you could look down the canal through all seven bridges. I was living on a tourist attraction. A couple of bridges down lived Tommy, his girlfriend Ann and Tracey. I soon settled into another glorious summer in Amsterdam.

The number 7 was a good place to work. As mentioned earlier it was in a flat above a small snack bar. Our two roulette tables were set up in what would have been the lounge. We had a kitchen for hot food, hot drinks and cold drinks. We had toilets and we had office space and a back room which at the time wasn't in use. Around the corner from us in the next alleyway was a small vegetarian restaurant called the Egg & Cream which did fantastic tuna and sweetcorn toasties and home made soups. I would often pop round on a break for my dinner or just to grab takeaways for the rest of the crew.

I was working with Jimmy Tong's crew that he had at the '217', Johan, Solo, Vivian and Juno amongst them. Big Chris the taxi driver was the katvanger. Tony Wu brought his family in with him. Marianne, his younger sister was a croupier, her older sister Wendy was employed to keep a watch over the tables, and another sister was a waitress. Slowly we employed some English croupiers. We had one couple join us called Alan and Julie. Julie was blonde with big blue eyes and rather slim. Alan was a joker. Everyday he would give us a new joke. Alan was one of those people who could remember hundreds of jokes and would often keep us laughing throughout the shift and well into the night at the bar.

It wasn't long before Big Henk found us and graced us with his presence. I remember one time he walked in with Big Pete, I assumed his bodyguard at the time. It was quiet so Henk had the roulette table to himself, just the way he liked it. I was dealing to him at the time and as usual taking him to the cleaners whilst he was cursing me in Dutch which by this time I was beginning to understand, but I let it go over my head.

Henk being a high roller attracted the attention of all the other gamblers in the place so it wasn't long before he had a crowd building up behind him. As I'd seen in the past Henk would usually grab a handful of five guilder notes from his pocket and throw them behind him to the 'peasants' to get rid of them. Only this time he just looked behind him with contempt and called across the casino to Big Pete who was sat quietly in a corner minding his own business.

On hearing his name being called Big Pete slowly rose up from his chair. Now Henk was a big guy and scary in himself but as Big Pete slowly rose he just seemed to get bigger and bigger. When Big Pete was at his full height he was about eight feet tall. Everything about him fitted. He had a big head with a big face. He needed specially made shoes to fit his feet and his hands were so big he could crush your skull with just one hand. He used to be a Dutch karate champion. I often wondered how he ever lost that title. He was big but he was gentle. He used to call me the 'Silver Fox' god knows why.

Now all these on lookers were mainly Chinese and Indonesian and all under five foot so when Big Pete was at full height and started to walk towards Henk all these little people just looked up at him and scampered like rats leaving a sinking ship.

We used to get so busy in the number 7 that sometimes I was literally surrounded by punters trying to put on bets. Usually roulette tables would be roped off to prevent punters from coming behind the tables and getting in your way but here at the number 7 they weren't. So I'd be dealing away and I'd have punters right up against me on my left or right and I'd have punters nipping around to my right or left getting bets down. It was quite hectic but fun.

We had one high roller who would come in and play roulette, nice guy. He'd play his game and when he did his brains he would come round the table take a seat and he would chip up for me, he loved it, he wasn't a bad chipper, he would add the bets up with me and pass over whatever I needed. Never once did he lift any cash chips when no one was looking.

He came in one night with a bag full of gold plated French lacquered Du Pont lighters. He told us they were fire damaged stock. We had no reason not to believe him though we weren't really bothered where they came from. Most of the crew bought one that night. He was asking for several hundred a piece and as we didn't have that sort of money on us Tony, the boss, ended up bankrolling us and coughed up the money. Of course we paid him back later.

I was dealing roulette one busy afternoon when this Surinam woman came in, her name was Marlene. We used to flirt and joke with each other so this one afternoon when she walked in I shouted something across the casino to her. She came back with a retort which I didn't hear so I asked her to repeat what she said. She came up close to the table and in front of everybody she said "I want to wash your dick." Well everybody around me just creased up with laughter and I was just stood there speechless and the colour of beetroot. Every time she came in after that I dreaded what she was going to come out with.

It was a busy afternoon in the number 7. Both roulette tables were going full tilt. I was dealing on one table and this new girl fresh in from England was on the other table. Big Henk decided to pay us a visit that afternoon. As I'd taken thousands of guilders of Henk over the years he took advantage of the situation and bought in on the other table.

It wasn't long before Henk's baritone voice filled the casino with abuse, the new girl was fleecing him. Fortunately she didn't know what he was calling her. When Henk started losing big he would get reckless with his gambling and start chasing his money. I was trying to concentrate on my own game but couldn't resist casting a glimpse over to the other table. On the occasion I looked over Henk had covered every number to the maximum except for zero. Now those out there in the business can guess what happened next, for those not in the business it's pretty obvious. The new girl span the ball and what comes in? Of course we all know, zero. The new girl starts to clear the layout apprehensively. By now she's feeling a bit nervous of this giant of a Dutchman in front of her.

As she cleared the layout Henk pulls out his semi automatic pistol from his shoulder holster and places it on zero with the barrel pointing at her. I'm watching this and notice the blood drain from her face and sense the fear she must be going through. "Henk." I shout across to him. He looks across to me sneering with an evil grin on his face. "Put the gun away, she's new in town you're scaring the shit out of her." Calling me a 'kanker roeder Englishman' he picks his gun up, holsters it and walks away giving me one of his standard evil looks.

Later after our shift we all went for a drink. The new girl was bought many drinks that night after her ordeal and she begins to understand the way of Amsterdam life.

CHAPTER TWENTY THREE
BUSTED

I was busted once when I was in Amsterdam. That was for possession of some mighty fine Paki Black hash. I was on my way to the Melkweg to pick up another couple of bags of this Paki Black when a street dealer asked me if I wanted to score some L.S.D. This must have been in early 1983 because I hadn't dropped any acid since my first New Years Eve in the city. I was interested so I made a mental note and continued to the Melkweg.

I scored my two bags of hash, had a drink at the bar then went in search of this street dealer. I found him propping up a tram stop. He was busy doing business so I hung back and waited until he was free. Suddenly three coppers pounced and the guy was spread eagled up against the tram stop while they frisked him. I turned and started walking away but one of the coppers called me back. Apart from the two bags of hash on me I was clean so I didn't do a runner, as far as I was concerned I wasn't breaking the law.

Before I knew it I was clapped in handcuffs and being marched off to the police station opposite the Melkweg. There I was head held high hands secured behind me purposely walking slowly towards the police station. The two coppers either side of me told me to walk faster, so I did. Too fast as it happened so they told me to slow down and walk properly. Not really a good idea to wind up coppers when you're clapped in irons.

Inside the police station on reception this street dealer was searched and they found all sorts of illegal substances on him. He was promptly booked and marched off to the cells. Now it was my turn. They asked me for identification so I produced my passport, I always carried it in case I got pulled in a casino raid. That way there was less likelihood of the police taking me to my flat for I.D. and them finding out I actually lived there. I was asked if I had any drugs on me, I said yes and produced the two bags of Paki Black hash thinking nothing of it. I asked them why I'd been picked up. They told me they thought I was working with this street dealer, I told them I didn't know him, they believed me. They asked me where I'd got the hash from and I told them across the road in the Melkweg. I didn't see the point in lying about it, the Melkweg was right across the road from them. They confiscated my hash and told me to strip right there and then on reception. There was nobody about so I stripped down to my underpants. They searched my pockets then told me to get dressed.

Then they just left me there sat on reception. After a while I got up and watched the football match being played on the TV with the some of the other coppers. At half time I asked them what was going to happen to me and they told me I would have to see the circuit judge who was due in town in a few days. I told them I was just a tourist and was due to go home the next day so they gave me a suspended fine of fifty guilders with a piece of paper with my name on it and the name of the arresting officer and told me to behave myself. I asked for my hash back and they just laughed and told me to be on my way. I left the police station went to another coffee shop scored some more hash then went round to tell Paul that I'd just been nicked.

Putting my arrest behind me we all settled into another glorious summer in the city. I continued to enjoy working at the number 7. Steve was still in his squat. Where I was living soon filled up with other croupiers and Tommy was still living down the road with Tracey.

Some time during the summer my old school friend Gary arrived back in Amsterdam. He'd come to stay after being involved and narrowly avoided being busted in a cocaine smuggling operation back in England. He soon settled down with me in my flat sleeping on my settee.

He needed to find work in order to survive. He used to be a croupier back in Sheffield but that wasn't his scene so we had to find something else for him to do. We sat down and discussed it and I suggested maybe he could become a porn star. He wasn't a bad looking lad and there was good money to be made. He came to the conclusion that videos were not a good idea. He still harboured dreams of becoming a famous drummer in a rock and roll band so we settled for photography work.

I told him I'd ask around and see what connections I could make. I didn't know anyone in particular in this line of business but I was sure I could ask around and get a contact. By the time I managed to get connected with someone in the porn industry Gary had already secured himself a job as a journalist with a new magazine portraying the cultural aspects of the city.

I would revel in my position as a 'Mr Fixit'. People just came to me for things or were sent by others. "Go and see Red, he hangs out at O'Henry's, he'll fix you up with whatever you need." They would be told. I would be propping up the bar in the English themed pub called O'Henry's on the Rokin when someone would come in and come up to me and ask me if I was 'Red'. No one called me Mark, I'd been nicknamed 'Red' by Theo at the '88' and it had stuck. So as they addressed me as Red someone must have sent them to see me.

As they were English it was odds on they were croupiers so I would ask them what I could do for them. It was the usual request, where can I find this, that or the other. Can you get me a job, find me a flat, where can I get some dope, coke, speed or acid or just another new croupier in town looking for an old friend of theirs. I had a reputation, which was well founded at the end of the day.

If it was a job they were after and I knew of one going I could send them straight to that casino. If I didn't know of a job going I could give them a list of casinos to visit with instructions on how to get there. If they were after accommodation I could usually furnish them with some names and addresses of landlords or letting agencies or point them in the right direction.

If it was drugs I could always send them to the coffee shops for the light stuff. For the heavy stuff then phone calls and introductions were warranted. If you were looking for an old friend then I would have to contact that person first before I gave them that persons whereabouts. A bit of this, that or the other took time but I would do my best.

A most unusual request came my way when Scott came over on one of his visits to see Kirstin. Scott bought a girl with him. I'll call her Mary. A very attractive young lady. I thought she was Scott's girlfriend.

We were all in O'Henrys having a few drinks. Mary was sat on one of the barstools in her tight jeans with her legs slightly apart. She kept putting her finger through a hole in the crotch of her jeans then sucking her finger.

After the third time of watching her do this the penny dropped and I asked Mary if there was anything I could do. She told me she was feeling really horny so I quickly suggested she come back to the flat with me. Mary declined my subtle offer, telling me she was a lesbian and she would like to find a girl. O.K. I thought. Here's a challenge so I put on my thinking cap.

I told Mary to come with me and we left everybody behind in O'Henrys. Outside I hailed a taxi and I took her to the Homolulu. Inside the Homolulu we took a seat at the bar and I got the drinks in. I told Mary to have a wander round and see if there was anyone she fancied. She didn't see anyone she fancied so we left the Homolulu and I took her to another gay club round the corner.

The club was quiet and Mary didn't see anyone to satisfy her carnal desires. All the time in the Homolulu and in this other club she kept diving her finger into the crotch of her jeans. For someone feeling really horny she was being a bit picky.

I wasn't going to be beaten so I spoke to one of the girls behind the bar and she gave me an address of a club just behind the

Rembrandts Plein. I'd never heard of this club which was no surprise as it was for women only. We got into another taxi and I took Mary to the club. She asked me if I was coming in and I told her I wouldn't be allowed entry as it was a women's club only. I wished her good luck and I never saw her again. I never did find out if I succeeded in getting a lesbian laid.

CHAPTER TWENTY FOUR
THE CABALA BURNS

December the 16th 1983, I was working the night shift at the number 7. It was a busy night on the tables. At about four a.m. Nina, a Swedish croupier came into the casino and came up to my table. She was very flustered and wanted to speak to Alan. I told her to slow down and calm down. I told her Alan wasn't working that night and asked her what the problem was.

After she managed to calm down she told me that the Cabala had caught fire and there were many casualties. This was not good news, the Cabala was one of the biggest casinos in the city. Nina told me what she could then left, still in a state of shock and panic. During the rest of the shift we gleaned as much information as we could from other punters coming and going.

When we closed at six a.m. we all went down to the Red Light district to see for ourselves. The district was alive with activity. The police and the fire brigade were still on the scene. People were everywhere, coming from all over the city to see the destruction of one of the city's most notorious gambling spots.

Being the middle of December the trees along the canal were covered in icicles from the fire hoses of the fire brigade. It was an eerie sight in the early hours of the morning. The bars were still open, they never closed that night. We went into one of the regular croupiers bars. It was full of stunned and shell shocked croupiers. Some from the

Cabala itself, others from surrounding casinos who had come to make sure friends and loved ones were safe.

The casualty list was high, thirteen dead and sixteen seriously wounded. Most of the staff who perished that night were Dutch. They were unfortunate to choose a fire exit that was blocked and wouldn't open and they died from smoke inhalation.

The fire was started by a guy called Joseph Lan an ex-doorman. He'd been in earlier and had a row with his ex-girlfriend who worked there. He was thrown out of the club only to return later with a jerry can of gasoline and a gun. As he entered the Cabala he sprinkled the gasoline up the entrance stairs as he went and used his gun to ignite the fire. He was later jailed. The old Cabala was torn down and apartments were built on the spot. At the base of the apartments a plaque sits in commemoration of the dead that night.

Years later an English croupier approached me in a bar and asked me if I remembered him. I must admit that I didn't but he told me he was working in the Cabala that night and he was pretty shaken up. He told me I stayed with him that morning buying him many brandy's to calm him down and he was grateful for that.

CHAPTER TWENTY FIVE
THE GOLDFISH BOWL

With Christmas and New Years Eve out of the way we slipped into 1984. Business at the number 7 is doing well. We are busy and the money keeps rolling in. I was working a night shift when Frank's son Peter walked into the casino with an English croupier called Phil.

Peter had organised with Tony and Jimmy to bring Phil in to give him a table test with the object of giving him a job in Yugoslavia for the winter Olympics. Phil did his table test and was offered the job. Peter had been watching me dealing roulette and he also offered me a job in Yugoslavia. I thanked him but declined the offer. I had a good steady job where I was and the winter Olympics didn't last for ever.

Tony and Jimmy liked the way Phil worked so they offered him a job with us which he accepted. Phil joined our crew and Peter walked away empty handed. Phil stayed working that night to get the hang of things and at the end of the shift we went out for a drink. I told him about the city and the casinos and gave him a phone number so he could fix himself up with a flat.

The next day I bumped into Tommy and Tracey. Tracey told me that she was off to Yugoslavia with Peter to work at the winter Olympics and would I like to move into the flat that she shared with Tommy. I jumped at the chance. I had been down to her flat several times. It was big, comfortable and would cost me less rent than my studio flat just up the road.

Gary had by this time moved out and got himself his own flat. Kirstin and Debbie were still there and there were plenty of other croupiers looking for a flat so when I moved out someone moved in and the landlord was kept happy. So I packed up my bags and moved myself into 68 Reguliersgracht with Tommy and his girlfriend Ann.

Number sixty eight was a ground floor flat. We had a large living room/kitchen. Out the back was the bathroom and a double bedroom where Tommy and Ann slept. Downstairs below street level was Tracey's bedroom, soon to be mine. You had to go through a smaller bedroom to get there. Back upstairs in the living room we had three large windows overlooking the Reguliersgracht and three large windows overlooking the Kerkstraat which ran all the way down to the Homolulu night club. We didn't possess curtains just some net curtains so Tommy had christened the flat 'The Goldfish Bowl'.

I settled myself into the flat. Tracey had flown off to Sarajevo for the Winter Olympics. It seemed as if she had just done a runner. The bed was unmade. She had two wardrobes of clothes, boxes of underwear and countless pairs of shoes lying all over the place. I boxed up all her clothes and shoes along with vast amounts of makeup and hung up my own stuff. Tracey had turned her bed into a four-poster with hanging lace, very feminine like. Her smell was strong in the bed so I didn't bother changing the sheets I just made the bed. When her lingering smell disappeared to be replaced by mine I changed the sheets.

Tommy was working in a casino on the Nieuwendijk for Franz, one of the Germans. I can't remember where Ann worked. Soon after I moved in Tommy and Ann split up, just leaving the two of us. We continued doing what we all did best. Working, drinking and smoking vast quantities of hash and grass. I was well into the cocaine, Tommy wasn't.

We were both earning good money so we decided to hire a cleaner twice a week. We were posh. She would come in and clean our mess, dust everything down and scrub clean our rather dirty kitchen and bathroom. Visitors couldn't believe how two hard working bachelors managed to keep the place so clean and tidy. They soon found out.

We had a steady stream of visitors coming round to see us. Liz was a regular. She would come round play backgammon and have a clean up round the flat. Liz was obsessionally tidy. Her flat was always spotless, and she took it upon herself to cook us meals, we weren't complaining. Another regular visitor was Helene, Peter's sister. Thick black curly hair, very pretty, cuddly and bubbly. She had a crush on Tommy which to my knowledge Tommy didn't reciprocate. He didn't dissuade her though because she would come round and cook us steak, egg and chips. One of Tommy's favourites. Tommy also introduced me to the wonders of tinned tomatoes on toast, another of his favourites.

Tommy also had a liking for the Rocky movies starring Sylvester Stallone. One day we were both on days off so he went to the video shop and hired all three Rocky movies. We parked our asses on the settee and watched Rocky one, two and three in succession and got stoned. When we finished watching Rocky three Tommy put Rocky one in the video and we settled down to watch them again. Told you Tommy had a liking for them.

Half way through watching Rocky two Tommy passed me the joint. As he did this a police car pulled up at the entrance to the Kerkstraat. The car was parked at an angle sealing off the street and the two police men inside were looking straight at me sat on the settee. Due to a plant by the window Tommy couldn't see the police car so I told him what was going on. He sat up, looked around the plant and instantly slouched back down into the settee. I went to pass Tommy the joint but paranoia had set in, he refused it.

I put the joint in the ashtray and let it go out. For the rest of the movie we both sat there not moving waiting for something to happen. We were both convinced we were going to be raided and carted off to jail. When Rocky two finished and there had been no movement from the police I got up and opened the window by the kitchen. I looked out at the police car and then down Kerkstraat. At the other end of the street was another police car parked the same way. Nothing was happening though, both police cars were just parked there sealing off the street. I told Tommy he could relax, they weren't here for us. He put Rocky three in the video and as he couldn't be seen because of the plant he rolled a joint. Tommy finished rolling the joint and the police started up and drove off and we could both relax again. Never did find out what they were up to.

Being lazy I used to jump out of the little window by the kitchen and nip across the road to this little shop. I'd come back with a crate of beers and pass them through to Tommy. Down the Kerkstraat on the corner of the Vijzelstraat was a small supermarket where we did most of our shopping. We were in there one day both stoned out of our brains.

Tommy had wandered off and I was stood admiring all the lovely coloured vegetables. Unbeknown to me Tommy had taken the trolley with him. This other guy had parked his trolley next to me and I started loading his trolley up with vegetables. When he thanked me for helping him with his shopping I cracked up with the giggles. When I found Tommy I told him what I'd done and as I couldn't control my fit of giggles we abandoned the shopping and went home for another joint.

Tommy's friend Steve came to stay with us. He took the spare bedroom downstairs next to mine. One day Tommy came home with some books about card counting. A technique to beat the house at blackjack. These books were rare and expensive at the time, you never saw them down at your regular bookshop. Steve and Tommy decided they wanted to get into card counting. They both stopped drinking and taking drugs so they could concentrate on the skills needed to become a good card counter. I was still enjoying myself too much so I just helped out.

Everyday after work instead of going out on the piss we all went home to learn. We'd got some green baize cloth from somewhere and draped it over the round dinner table we had in the front room. We had

106

a shoe and some chips and I would deal blackjack to them for hours on end. Every time Tommy came home with more books I would take them round the corner to this shop who would print off three copies for me. I later found out the guy was printing off four, one for himself.

Liz would still come round and tidy for us. One day we all had to go out and we left Liz behind to clean up. We told her she could tidy anything she wanted but not to touch our dinning room table. It may have looked a mess but it was our mess and we knew where to find everything. When we got home Liz had ignored our instructions and all our books, charts and notes were nicely piled up. Such is life.

One day Big Chris took Phil and me into the attic of the number 7. He unlocked a door and we followed him up a steep and winding dusty staircase. At the top we came into a maze of empty dusty rooms. Like the staircase, the walls weren't plastered just bare wooden slats. We followed Big Chris as he led us through room after room with bare bricked walls and staircases leading down to somewhere. When we looked through a window down on to the alleyway we realised we were several buildings up from the number 7. We had just walked through all the attics of the shops and houses along the Nieuwezijds Kolksteeg. All that empty space just sitting there. I wondered how many people knew these places existed.

About a week after Big Chris gave us a guided tour of the attics Tony opened up the back room and installed a Chinese game. I think it was called Pi Kow. It was a very simple game played on a table about the size of a Baccarat table. It attracted a lot of money and was a big hit with the Chinese. Tony allowed us to play the game. A big pile of little white beads were placed in the middle of the table. A small tub was put on top of them and a portion of beads were siphoned off from the big pile. Once this was done bets were placed on the numbers one to four. With all bets down the tub was removed from the pile and the Chinese dealer using a small stick would count off four beads at a time. The last remaining beads denoted the winning bet. So if you had a hundred guilders on number three and three beads were remaining then you won. All bets were paid out at even money. Told you it was simple.

April the 30th, Queens Day was upon us. As usual the streets were packed and getting to work was a nightmare. Big Chris was late turning up so one of the croupiers went and bought a whole chocolate hash cake. Everybody had a slice except me. Someone had to stay compis mentis. Tony's sister Marianne even helped herself to a slice. She never took drugs and she thought it was an ordinary chocolate cake. Nobody told her any different.

About an hour later Big Chris eventually arrived and unlocked the doors and we got down to business. Marianne opened up the roulette table. After about an hour she had a great big grin on her face and was clearly enjoying herself. After two hours it became clear she was having difficulty adding up her bets. When Marianne was beginning to find it hard to put her dolly on the winning number I had her taken off and told her to go for a break. She went over to the settee in the corner for a lay down and promptly fell asleep. She slept through the rest of the shift and she never did find out she'd eaten a slice of hash cake.

Protection in the city was run by Bart Van Veen. His 'boys' were everywhere. In the Red Light district protecting the hookers, on the doors of sex clubs, strip joints, bars and nightclubs. If you needed or wanted protection then Bart was the man. Sometimes even if you didn't want it you got it, of course at a price. Sometimes the casinos would only need one or two guys to cover the door. Not all our doormen were hired from Bart but they were all connected in one way or another.

It was handy knowing these guys. They would get us into nightclubs without paying or queuing. If anyone had any grief on the street we only had to go to the nearest 'door' for protection. Not that many of us had any problems. When people realised who we were and who we worked for, unless we were looking for trouble, no one bothered us.

Some time in March Tommy came home from work one evening and told me a story of an incident that had happened that afternoon in the casino where he worked.

This guy came into the casino and lost a lot of money on the blackjack table. He got pissed off and hit the croupier in his frustration then walked out the casino. The next thing I see are about half a dozen big mean looking geezers enter the casino and go into the office. About twenty minutes later they lumber out the office and the casino.

They were out on the streets scouring the casino's looking for this guy. They knew who he was and the likely places to find him. They eventually found him on the top floor of this casino which was situated on the edge of the Red Light district. Four storeys high with steep narrow stairs.

They got hold of this guy and threw him down all four flights of stairs. When he got to the bottom he was battered and bruised with a few broken bones. He was then dragged out onto the street and in front of all theses tourists milling around one of the guys pulled a gun, cocked it and put it to his head telling him that if he ever did that again it would be the last thing he ever did.

Moral of the story. Always stay friendly with 'the entertainments committee'.

By the time I moved in with Tommy I was well into cocaine. I knew most of the night clubs where I could go and 'chat' to the man sat at the end of the bar. I also knew a few dealers where I could give them a phone call and go round to their flat for some gear.

One day I went round to see Jan, my coke dealer at the time. He only lived a few streets away. His girl friend was out so it was just him and me. Jan asked me if I wanted to try some 'freebase'. Now I'd heard about it but never tried it so I thought I'd give it ago.

Jan measured out a gram of coke and two grams of baking powder and poured it into a glass test tube. He added an amount of water then gently heated it over an open flame on his gas cooker. The water boiled off leaving behind some hard glittering crystals of pure cocaine.

These hard crystals of cocaine cannot be snorted, they'd rip your nose to shreds and you wouldn't get the full benefit anyway. Jan produced a special glass pipe and I smoked my first freebase. It was an instant high but a short lived high. I understood why it was so addictive after a few hits. So I was eternally grateful that I never properly learned the process of making freebase.

When I wasn't eating at the Egg & Cream I would nip downstairs to the snack bar beneath the number 7. I was down there one winter's afternoon when the police decided to raid us. I sat there finishing my meal watching them through the window trying to gain entry. They were still there when I finished eating and paid my bill. I left the snack bar and went round the corner to this bar that was being run by an Egyptian poker dealer called Ben. I told him we were being raided so he went out to have a look. He came back and told me they were still trying to get in. We had a drink and then he went out for another look. This time he came back and told me they had gained entry. After another drink I went out to see what was happening. A crowd had gathered to watch the action. Punters and croupiers were coming out the door and no one seemed to be getting arrested. I'd left my coat upstairs and when I saw Phil he offered to go back in and get it for me. I didn't fancy going in myself in case I got nicked. Then number 7 was locked up and all the croupiers went out for the usual post raid piss up.

Occasionally I would hop on a plane and fly home to visit my parents who lived in Southend-on Sea. I could get a direct flight from

Schipol airport to Southend airport. Because of the one hour time difference I'd ring up my mother and tell her I was leaving Amsterdam at two o'clock and to have the kettle on at two fifteen. Ross would pick me up at the airport and drive me home. I would stay for a couple of days and tell them stories of my exciting adventures in Amsterdam.

On one of our drives back to the airport to get my return flight Ross told me that some of the stories I was coming out with were beginning to worry Pat, my mother, and he asked me to tone them down a bit. So there are some things I never told you mother, until now.

In August Tommy left Amsterdam to go and work in Germany. Liz was also going to Germany so we gave up the 'Goldfish Bowl' and I moved into Liz's flat on the Paardenstraat round the corner from the Rembrandts Plein. Around this time I started going out with Kim. Kim, like me, enjoyed her whisky and we would often get up and go to this pub in the Rembrandts Plein and have a couple of double whisky's for breakfast before going home and back to bed.

November came and it was my twenty fifth birthday. Croupiers from all over the city came round to the flat each of them bringing a bottle of Champagne. As you can imagine the night was a blur. Next morning after breakfast I counted twenty five empty bottles of Champagne lying around the flat.

That winter was an extremely cold one. It was so severe the canals and the inner seas in Holland froze over. In the north of Holland in a place called Friesland they held large ice skating races. Seeing the canals frozen over in Amsterdam was quite an amazing sight. Suddenly all these people appeared skating up and down the canals. Residents of the house boats on opposite sides of the canal suddenly became sociable and impromptu parties would begin.

One day Phil and I were trundling through the snow on the way to work when Phil though it a good idea to take a short cut over the canal. With Phil being heavier than me I thought it best to let him go first and test the strength of the ice. As he gingerly set off across the ice I walked round over the bridge and met him on the other side in one piece, dry and safe.

Being out of work I gave up the flat on Paardenstraat and flew home for a couple of weeks and stayed with Kim in her flat in London. I soon got a phone call telling me that Tony Wu was opening a new casino and I had a job waiting for me. We both flew back to Amsterdam. Kim got a job in Germany while I stayed in Amsterdam and moved into a flat on the Langestraat.

CHAPTER TWENTY SIX
VIDEOS, HOOKERS AND GOING FOR A BEER

The number 5 was one big room with an office out back, a small kitchen area in the corner and toilets downstairs in the basement. Chris was the katvanger and most of the crew from the number 7 teamed up again to work for Tony Wu. We had two American roulette tables, two blackjack tables, a poker table and a couple of tables at the end of the room for a couple of Chinese games.

There were several tables dotted about the place for punters to play Kalooki or Mah Jong. In one corner we had a television and video system set up with a couple of settees for lounging on. We always kept plenty of rented videos on the premises for the punters to chill out and watch. Most of them were action movies such as war movies, gangster movies and it being mainly a Chinese casino plenty of martial arts movies.

Once a month we would take the videos back to the shop and get in a fresh batch. I would always volunteer for this thankless job of going out and choosing another twenty to thirty videos for the coming month. The video shop was situated on the edge of the Red Light district. I would stroll over and browse the shelves and choose a selection of movies.

Job done I would then take the long road back to the casino through the Red Light district taking in the sights of the girls in the windows and stopping off in a bar for a beer and no doubt a chat with someone I knew. Of course by the time I got back to work there were the usual accusations that I had stopped off and tasted the delights of one of the girls, but as usual they were wrong. That would be taking the piss.

Working in the number 5 during the summer was a delight. Out of the door, down the alley way and across the street were two bars. When the casino was quiet and there weren't any major players about I would ask Tony's sister Wendy, if it was ok if I could nip out for a beer. Knowing I wouldn't take the piss she always said yes.

I would saunter out across the road order myself a beer, and take a table outside so I could see the door to the casino and note who was coming and going. When any major punter entered the casino I would knock back my beer, head back to the casino and get my ass back on the roulette table. Wendy always noticed my promptness hence her being agreeable to me going for a beer. As for my bar bill when I finished my shift I would go over to whichever bar I was in and settle up.

In April this couple called Arif and Anya opened a bar on the Nieuwezijds Voorburgwal just round the corner from the number 5. They called it the Bar Felicita. I'd met Arif before when he worked as a barman in a bar just off the Red Light district. The Bar Felicita was in the basement of a house. Walking down the steps you enter the bar which was long and narrow with no windows. There was no fire exit and out the back were two toilets and a store room.

Next door to the Bar Felicita was a Turkish restaurant. It was a big place with plenty of tables and always busy. In the rafters of the ceiling were hundreds of boxes that used to contain bottles of Chivas Regal, a mighty fine blended whisky. Arif told me he was a friend of the owner and he only drank Chivas Regal and every time he finished a bottle the box went up in the ceiling. The restaurant did a nice mixed grill and I would often pop in and get one for a take away and eat it back in the casino.

I was getting heavily into cocaine at this time and drinking a lot as well. Working the day shift didn't help much as it meant my evenings were free to party all night long. I would often wake up the next day with no recollection of the night before. Fortunately Arif's wife Anja had an amazing memory. I would go back to the bar the next day and she could tell me what I was drinking, how much my bar bill was, who I was talking too and about what and whether or not I'd upset anybody. As she told me things my memory slowly came back to me.

During an afternoon shift this regular Italian punter came in. He'd been doing his brains and he came in with some stuff to sell. He had a collection of silver coins which Marianne got to first but he also had a couple of volumes of first day cover Italian stamps from the sixties and seventies which I quickly bought off him.

It was during that same shift when I found out I'd won two and a half thousand guilders on the illegal lottery. Eve and I had done a combination of numbers with Indonesian Alex and our numbers came in. To put in my claim I had to track the elusive Alex down and it still wasn't until a couple of weeks later that he finally coughed up our winnings.

After work I took my collection of Italian stamps home for safe keeping then went back to Arif's. It was quiet in the bar so Arif took the opportunity to offer me an original international driver's licence. He had ten for sale at the time. Now I could drive after a fashion, but I'd never been licensed so owning one of these was an interesting prospect. Arif was asking for a thousand guilders per licence. I told him I'd take one but unfortunately he was selling them as a job lot. I didn't have ten grand at the time and besides, I didn't really want to be lumbered with ten international driver's licences so I had to decline the offer.

The next day I went to meet Kim at the railway station. She'd just flown in from London. She'd met a guy on the plane who had tried chatting her up. His name was Bernie and he was from New Zealand. Bernie had Dutch relatives, he was over six foot tall with short brown hair. We directed him to some hotels and I gave him my address and told him to come round when he got settled in.

Bernie turned up the next day and we showed him around the city. He'd decided he was going to stay in Amsterdam and he soon went out and bought himself a car. It wasn't long before we were tootling all over the city smoking dope and playing loud music with the windows rolled down.

A few days after meeting Bernie he turned up at the flat. He'd done a drawing for me of the devil snorting cocaine off his tongue. He said I'd given him the idea. Bernie first and foremost was a mechanic but he was also quite an artist.

CHAPTER TWENTY SEVEN
AMERICAN WHEELS

When I was working at the '88' I dealt a lot of American roulette. We used the old style French wheel which was heavy and solid, unlike today's modern American wheels which are light and flimsy. Over time with continuous use I developed my own technique of controlling the wheel. A lot of punters would play one of two sections on the wheel. I would let them place their bets and depending on which section was most heavily backed I would spin the opposite section.

I was able to do this by spinning the ball and the wheel at a certain speed. It's not a technique easily learnt. I couldn't control my spin on a reverse spin so I would lean over the wheel and always do a normal spin. Over the years my reverse spin became weak much to the amusement of other croupiers when I returned to working in English casinos.

Not many people believed I could do what I said I could do but I was pretty confident I could place the ball in any of the two sections eight out of ten times. I had to be subtle when glancing down the layout before spinning. I got away with this method for many years. I later tried this method with the American wheels but as mentioned before they were just too light and flimsy to have any control over them.

I continued to hone my technique at the number 7 so by the time I ended up working for Tony Wu in the number 5 I was a master of my art. When I was on form I would end up working a whole shift behind a roulette table. I would eat drink and smoke behind the table. If I didn't have time to eat I would get one of the waitresses to bring me a glass of milk with two raw eggs whisked in it. I would gulp that down and continue fleecing the punters. When I was on fire sometimes I would tell Big Chris, the katvanger, to bring me a double brandy and coke to keep me going. If I needed to go to the toilet I would spin the ball and run downstairs whilst my chipper would take over. By the time I got back he would be paying out any winning bets and I would step back in and take over again.

We had two American roulette tables in the number 5 next to each other. When both tables were in full swing I would stand between them and spin both balls letting someone else deal the game. Knowing how certain people played I would set up the payouts, subtly including low value cash chips so they ended up betting more each spin. Lucy, one of the English croupiers, came into the number 5 one day and she later told me she was amazed to watch me in action as she'd never seen anything like it before. I got pretty good at dealing roulette so much so that one day in O'Henry's bar Jerry and Eric voted me the best wheel man in town. Coming from those two that was a serious compliment.

Being able to manipulate a French roulette wheel when working came in handy for when I wasn't working. Being in the business I wasn't a gambler but on my travels around the other casinos I soon found out that I could read other croupiers spins and realised I could make some money. So every night after work I would cross the road to the '217' run by Jimmy Tong and his crew. My standard operating procedure was as follows.

I would go in with the intention of spending one hundred guilders only. I would play sections of the wheel. If I started winning and I ended up with two hundred guilders in front of me I would take my original one hundred guilder buy in and put it back in my pocket and play with what I had left. When I had another two hundred guilders in front of me I would take a hundred guilders and put that in my pocket. Now I was winning a hundred guilders. I would continue playing with what I had left. Every time I had a hundred guilders in front of me I would bank it and keep playing until my remaining chips were gone. I never got greedy and upped my stakes. On average I was winning five to seven hundred guilders a week on top of my wages.

Sometimes, when I was on a run, I would do a tour of the casinos picking up a few hundred here and there. Sometimes I would just alternate casinos so as not to piss the bosses off. Just about every night I would return to the Bar Felicita and ring the bell. This meant drinks all round. The guys couldn't believe it when I did it three nights on the trot. It pissed the Chinese off as well. There I was cleaning them out during the day then going out gambling and coming back a winner just about every night.

My flat on the Langestraat was a nice one. I had a living room with a partitioned kitchen and a double bedroom out the back. My bathroom was small with an unusual half sized weird shaped bath with a shower over the top. Above the living room up a ladder was a low crawl space which was quiet large and sometimes doubled up as a spare bedroom when I had guests.

At the time Paul was concerned about my cocaine intake. He used to take my coke off me and test it. If it was bad stuff he'd flush it down the toilet. He was in my kitchen one day doing a heat test using some tin foil on my latest batch of cocaine. The cocaine suddenly exploded giving off a bluish flame and lots of black stuff ended up floating in the air. Whatever it was quickly disappeared down the toilet.

CHAPTER TWENTY EIGHT
MDMA THE NEW DRUG IN TOWN

It was sometime in May, it was my day off. I was wandering around the city aimlessly checking out friends, bars and shops. Come late afternoon I strolled in the Bar Felicita to see Arif. As I walked through the door I noticed there were an unusual number of Chinese in already. I walked down the length of the bar, took a seat in the corner and ordered a beer. I then took in my immediate surroundings.

At my end of the bar were a few of the regular Chinese that hung out with us croupiers. Along the length of the bar sat some more of the Chinese lads and at the other end of the bar sat another bunch of lads, nationality unknown. The atmosphere was tense. Suddenly it clicked, I'd just walked into a major drugs deal.

A couple of the top Chinese boys were present. Those that regularly carried guns were also present. Negotiations were taking place in the middle of the bar between both parties. I was out of place but I wasn't going to get up and leave. This was my regular bar and the Chinese knew it. They bought me another beer and some of them not immediately involved engaged me in conversation. I didn't ask them about their business, even though it was obvious.

Some of the Chinese boys left and shortly reappeared carrying packages under their jackets. Bundles of what I assumed were cash were exchanged and once satisfied the guys at the end of the bar got up and left. The atmosphere suddenly became relaxed.

Chinese Andrew came down to the end of the bar where I was sat and handed Arif several hundred guilder notes. I guess that was his payoff for allowing his bar to be used for doing business. He placed another hundred on the bar and told Arif that was for my bar bill then he left with some of the other Chinese boys. A few of the boys stayed behind and during the course of the evening the place filled up with croupiers and we all got drunk until closing time.

A couple of weeks later on my day off I once again ended up at the Bar Felicita. It was a quiet afternoon, Arif was at the end of the bar talking to a stranger so I took a seat at the end of the bar by the door and ordered a beer. It wasn't long before Arif sent the stranger down the bar to me. "He wants to do some business Red so I told him to speak to you." Arif informed me as he put another beer and a double scotch in front of me.

I introduced myself and he told me his name was George. "How can I help?" I asked him as I shook his hand. George informed me he had just flown in from America and he was in Europe to do some business. "What sort of business?" I asked him. He opened his brief case and handed me an envelope. I looked inside and saw several white pills about the size of an aspirin. "LSD?" I asked looking up at him. "No not LSD, MDMA, it's a new drug from America known on the streets as Ecstasy. MDMA is its chemical name." He explained. "What does it do?" I asked him. George told me it was similar to LSD but without the hallucinations and similar to cocaine but lasted longer.

He told me one pill would last several hours and it would get me high and make me feel very happy.

I'd taken LSD and was well into cocaine so I was intrigued. George told me a bit more about the drug and its chemical breakdown. "So how can I be of assistance?" I asked him.

"I've got a large supply and I'm looking for distributors." He told me. Now I've done a few drug deals in my time but I'm no major drug dealer but I knew several people who were.

"How many have you got with you?" I asked him.

"How many do you want?" he asked me.

"Leave me a hundred and I'll distribute them to some of my people and if we like what you've got we'll talk business." I said.

"I can't leave you a sample you have to buy them." he said. George just made his first mistake.

"It doesn't work like that George. I don't know how you do things in America but this is Amsterdam and what you're offering is a new drug. If you want to do business you leave me a sample. If what you're offering is as good as you say it is I can put you in contact with people who can move thousands of these."

"I can't do that." George said.

"In that case this interview is over." I told him. George put his envelope back in his briefcase and left the bar never to be seen again. I figure he must have made the right connections because Ecstasy went on to be a best seller, still is today.

CHAPTER TWENTY NINE
EIGHT COLOURS AND A CALCULATOR

The summer of '85 was another hot one. The number 5 was busy and successful. It was non stop from the moment we opened. I was on permanent day shift which left my evenings free for some serious drinking. Tony had put all the croupiers on a 10% bonus for every fifty thousand guilders we won. Most weeks we were looking at picking up that bonus twice a week, sometimes, though rarely, three times a week. We were all fired up, on form and rolling in cash.

My strongest game at the time was American roulette so I always seemed to be there doing what I did best. Eight colours, two hundred chips per colour, sixteen hundred chips per spin, including cash chips and cash call bets. Day in day out, hour after hour. I was good at constantly calculating and paying out bets with speed and precision. Nobody doubted whether the payout was correct or not.

One afternoon I was dealing to these two giant Indonesians. For Indonesians these guys were BIG and they were doing their brains. They questioned one of my payouts saying it was incorrect so I re-calculated and told them the payout was correct. They still weren't happy and demanded I try again. Now I wasn't happy and was just about to make a comment when one of our regular punters looked up at them and said "If the Red man says it's correct it's correct." They soon shut up and continued to lose their chips and more cash.

Every afternoon I would end up dealing to the regular gang of Chinese boys. The same gang I would get drunk and stoned with the night before. They were high rollers and took their losses like gentleman. These guys liked to play the zero section a lot and when I hit twenty nine or thirty two which was always plastered with chips, cash chips and cash they would all add up the bets to make sure I got them right. Often, when possible, I would add up the biggest bet on the table before the ball dropped giving me an advantage if I should hit that number.

Every day I'd hit these bets and every day I'd get them right which would frustrate the Chinese boys as they were always trying to catch me out. So it was no surprise when one afternoon after hitting thirty two which was piled high with chips one of the Chinese boys pulled out a calculator and began to check my bets. Much to the amusement of the rest of the table we got to work and he confirmed my bets as being correct by showing all the others the figure he had on his calculator.

The next day the game was just the same and I was in full swing. The cast of Chinese were the same and the verbals in English and Chinese were flying back and forth, all in good humour. It had to happen and sure enough the ball dropped into twenty nine, the biggest bet on the layout. I cleared the table and opened the bet to start paying out. I stepped back to begin the task before me and as I did so half a dozen Chinese boys also stepped back and they all pulled their own calculators from their pockets. The heat was on but I wasn't fazed.

It was no surprise when the next day the ivory ball found thirty two. Everyone around the table started laughing, took one step back and they all pulled out calculators. The sound of fingers tapping on keys filled the air as I slowly opened the bets ready for adding up. They were all stood there around the table making their calculations and showing each others their calculators and looking at me with a challenge in their eyes. I took one step back from the table looked at the bet as if ready to start adding it up then reached into my back pocket and pulled out my own calculator. Amidst a roar of laughter I totted up the bet and showed everybody the figure on my calculator which conferred with theirs. After that I never saw another calculator in the casino again.

A few days later it was another hot summer's day. Inside the casino it was hot, smoky and packed with gamblers. Both roulette tables were buzzing with action. The usual eight colours, two hundred chips per colour, sixteen hundred chips per spin, cash chips appearing across the layout and vast amounts of cash flying in from all sides. Glad I wasn't dealing, god help the chipper if he was slow.

This day I was having a day off. I was dealing on the blackjack table. One of two across the casino opposite the roulette tables. To my right the television was on, showing the usual Chinese kung fu movie. A group of Chinese boys were lounging about on the settee nattering away about god knows what. Over in the corner the poker table was also seeing some action. The game had been going on since the night before. People of all nationalities were milling about the place, wheeling and dealing and trying to borrow some more money to get back into the action.

Both blackjack tables were ticking over nicely, everyone was cool and relaxed. I had three regulars playing the table placing irregular stacks of ten guilder chips on five boxes. I was winning, they were losing, but still they would dig deeper into their pockets bringing out obscene amounts of cash in a mixture of different currencies.

Out of the crowd loomed this rather large Pakistani. I'd never seen him before and I knew most of the gamblers in town. He approached my table and threw a wad of hundred guilder notes down on the layout in front of me. I gathered the money up and counted it out in front of me at the same time asking him how he would like it. "All in tens." He barked at me, his cocaine fuelled eyes staring down at me. "Fifteen hundred." I said, assessing my float. I reached in and lifted out thirty ten guilder chips and cut them down in front of me.

"No all tens." He said. Cutting down twenty four fifty guilder chips I explained to him that I had a game going on and I needed to keep some tens in the float in order to pay out.

"I want all tens." He barked back at me.

My three regulars on the table were sensing the tension. Knowing me they looked at him with contempt for disturbing their game and then at me as if to say 'what are you going to do with this one then?' I looked up at the big Pakistani with his cocaine eyes and said "Fuck off." He looked at me stunned at my bluntness.

"What did you say?" he said, giving me the evil eye.

"You heard me, fuck off." I said knowing that any trouble would soon be dealt with. My regulars carried guns and were not afraid to flash them to make a point.

"Where's the boss?" he asked me menacingly.

"In the office, over there." I pointed across the casino behind the roulette tables.

He steamed off in a huff and I changed his chips up into hundreds and put them to one side. I continued dealing blackjack. People still milled through the smoky haze, skin smacked against skin on the television and the sound of ivory balls spinning drifted over from the roulette tables.

A couple of shoes later the big Pakistani walked out of the office with Big Chris close on his heels. They both approached the table. "What's going on over her?" he asked me. I explained to Chris the nature of the problem. He listened, looked at the big Pakistani and said "Cash in your chips and fuck off." The big man didn't argue he cashed in his chips and without a word quietly left the casino and I made another twenty one.

One afternoon we had an incident in the club. I can't remember what it was about. After our shift we went to Arif's for a drink. It was the height of the summer and the tables and chairs were out on the pavement. We were joined by some other croupiers and I went inside to get a round of drinks in. When I came out with a tray of drinks Debbie was telling the story of that afternoon's incident. I stood behind Debbie and listened to her tell the tale. When she finished I put the tray down and told her crowd of listeners that what she'd just told them was a total fabrication. Debbie was a bit miffed at this so I told everyone exactly what happened. It was amazing how Debbie could get it all wrong when the incident only happened a few hours earlier and we were both stood side by side at the time.

With Kim in Germany and me in Amsterdam we soon split up. I moved out of my flat on the Langestraat and moved in with Phil, Debbie and Wendy on the Nieuwezijds Voorburgwal opposite the Corner House Hotel. Phil and Debbie were an item and took one double bedroom and Wendy and I shared the other double bedroom. As much as I wanted Wendy and me to be an item we weren't so we had separate single beds. Like Debbie Wendy was Welsh. She was a skinny little thing with short blond hair and blue eyes and like me an avid reader. That's probably what attracted me to her, she was intelligent.

The Corner House Hotel had a nice downstairs bar and apart from the tourists coming and going it had a regular clientele and it became one of my regular watering holes. A bonus came with the Corner House in the name of Cathy. She was an English croupier and she had a permanent room in the hotel. Long brown hair with these big brown eyes. She was a little older than I was and as her husband wasn't around much I would occasionally spend the night with her.

CHAPTER THIRTY
LOOKING FOR GUNS

The calculators were gone but I was still getting involved in schemes which in my eyes were calculated to be successful. It all started one hot July afternoon. We were having a slow time in the casino this one particular afternoon so I took time out and went across the road for a drink. I got myself a cold beer, grabbed a boiled egg off the bar and ordered a sandwich.

Sat outside in the sun with a view of the casino door I relaxed and enjoyed my ice cold beer. A couple of the Chinese boys turned up and came over to join me. They got a round of drinks in and we got chatting. I asked them if they could lay their hands on any opium. I'd smoked some once back in England and I figured if anyone could get some these guys could. I was to be disappointed. They told me the smuggling of opium stopped many years ago as it was too bulky, too aromatic and didn't generate the sort of revenue that heroin did.

I was diving into my brie and grape sandwich and supping on my second beer when it was their turn to ask me for a favour. They explained that they were having a bit of a problem with a rival gang of Chinese and asked me if I could lay my hands on some guns for them. I was a bit surprised at the request, these guys were always tooled up and I expressed the opinion that surely they had better contacts than me. They told me they didn't want to go through their usual contacts as it would alert their intentions to their rivals, so finishing my sandwich and beer I told them I'd see what I could do for them. Together all three of us walked back to the casino and I went back to work.

I'd never been approached for guns before but I liked a challenge. I wasn't sure who to broach the subject with but I did have a few people in mind who I could trust to be discreet. I figured if I could pull this little number off it would put me in good with the Chinese and I could either make a few bucks out of the deal or even pick up a piece for myself or even both.

A couple of days later on a Saturday night I was in the Homolulu. It was a very busy night. A lot of casino staff, bosses, punters and some civilians were all having a good time. I was in the restaurant polishing of an excellent beef stroganoff when I noticed the man I was looking for propping up the bar with a couple of beauties. I caught his eye and motioned for him to lose the women while I had a chat. I approached him at the bar. "What can I do for you Red man?" he asked, or rather shouted in my ear. Don't forget we were in a busy nightclub on a Saturday night.

"I'm looking for some hardware." I shouted back in his ear.

"What sort of hardware?" he asked.

"About half a dozen revolvers, half a dozen semi-automatics with a hundred rounds a piece, how much?" I asked. I waited a couple of minutes while his brain did some quick calculations.

"No problem, I can do the revolvers for five hundred a piece and the semi's for seven-fifty, that's including the ammo."

"Ok sounds good. I'll have to get back to you on this." I turned to leave him to get back to his girls at the bar but I'd forgotten something so I turned back to him and shouted into his ear if he could also get some hand grenades. "HAND GRENADES" were the two words to spill from his mouth that filled the Homolulu as suddenly the music stopped. As people around the bar turned to stare I melted into the crowd and became scarce.

The next day I met up with the Chinese boys and gave them some figures. They thanked me but explained that their little problem had been worked out diplomatically and there was no need for bloodshed. So I never did mange to pull off that tasty little number.

CHAPTER THIRTY ONE
THE NIGHT I GASSED BERNIES CAR

It was just another typical July night down in the Bar Felicita. The place was jumping. Several locals were in, the usual gang of Chinese were present and a whole bunch of croupiers. Earlier in the evening I was sat down at the end of the bar with Phil, Debbie, Steve, Bernie and Robbie. Robbie was a scouser, like Alan had a head full of jokes and was always up for a laugh. He always claimed to be related to General Bernard Montgomery. Robbie was sat in front of me with his head buried in the Sun newspaper. I'd just lit up a Gitane cigarette and before putting my Zippo back in my pocket I put the flame to the bottom of the newspaper. The Sun burst into flames before Robbie's eyes. He was quick to throw the burning newspaper to the floor and stamp out the flames. Small pieces of charred remains of the Sun floated around us. Phil, Debbie and Steve were not impressed. Bernie and Robbie were laughing away hysterically.

Phil and Debbie decided to go out for a meal shortly after that incident and the bar began to fill up. Alan and his wife Julie came in after finishing their shift along with Sian. Wendy joined us along with Gerry, Karen, Squatter Steve and a whole lot of others from the other casinos round town. We all got drunk and stoned and later in the wee hours of the morning when only the English croupiers were left vast quantities of cocaine was sniffed off Arif's copy of the yellow pages at the bar.

Come closing time we helped Arif clean up and put the stools up on the bar out of the way. Bernie decided to come back to the flat to continue partying. I'd forgotten Bernie had his car with him. Instead of leaving it he decided to drive to the flat which was only about thirty five meters away. I decided to walk so headed off before he started the car.

As I was crossing the road to the flat Bernie was just pulling up at the kerb. Being a bit drunk, stoned and wired I decided to have a bit of fun. I walked up to the car and tapped on Bernie's window. As Bernie wound down his window I reached into the top right hand pocket of my jacket and pulled out my can of C.S. gas and proceeded to give Bernie a good gassing, or so I thought.

Bernie, seeing this action, and knowing what I kept in that particular pocket instinctively ducked thus avoiding my sudden drunken gas attack. When his car door opened and out stepped Bernie, all six foot plus of him, not showing any signs of being gassed I knew I was in trouble. What followed was like something out of an old black and white silent movie. Bernie started to chase me round the car. As he's chasing me I'm telling him not to come close as I was still armed with a full can of C.S. gas. As this was going on, to my surprise and horror three other bodies came falling out of Bernie's car. Showing obvious signs of having taken the full brunt of the gas attack. They weren't a threat but Bernie was and he was getting closer. My only course of action was to get inside quick and to safety. So with keys at the ready I made for the front door.

With all the commotion going on my flat mates Debbie and Phil, two floors up, had opened the window to investigate. As they were hanging out the window witnessing all this I managed to get my key in the door at the same time as Bernie caught up with me. He lifted me up of the pavement and started swinging me around. I was laughing like a lunatic and let off another long burst of C.S. gas.

Bernie caught a face full of gas and dropped me. I made for the door, got the key in the lock and I got inside to safety. I secured the door behind me and ran up the stairs and let myself into the flat. Locking the door behind me I ran into the living room only to find that Phil and Debbie whilst hanging out the window had also suffered from the last burst of gas rising into the night air. After a few choice words from Debbie, and Phil seeing the funny side of things I went to bed and slept peacefully. Bernie took Wendy back to his flat to take care of her.

The next day I thought it best to search out and apologise to the three bodies in the car who had suffered the full brunt of the C.S. gas attack. I didn't find them until later in the day. Whilst I was out they had come looking for me. As I wasn't home they took my camera and drove off to Zandvoort beach for the day and used up all my film.

When I did catch up with them in the evening I made my apologies to Sian, Wendy and Steve who were in the car. Phil and Debbie from the flat, and I made my peace with Bernie, who like Phil, also saw the funny side of things.

CHAPTER THIRTY TWO
GRAND THEFT BICYCLE

The long hot summer was coming to an end. The leaves were falling from the trees as we slipped into autumn. The Bar Felicita was thriving. Not only was it busy with the crew from the number 5 and the '217' but croupiers from other casinos would also turn up to party.

Most of our Chinese punters would also hang out with us. By day we would take their money, by night we would get stoned and drunk with them. Several local people would also hang out with us. There were two bars across the road from us. Their owners knew Arif so they would pop in for a drink. There was a couple who owned a stamp shop around the corner and between the two bars was a little shop run by a jeweller.

With my pockets full of cash I got into buying jewellery. Whether it was gold chains, rings, bracelets, diamonds or other precious stones I would take the item into his shop before handing over any money and he would do his little tests and authenticate it for me. Unless I wanted any major work done, like repairs, he never charged me for all the little tests he carried out.

It was like being in a western when you were in the Bar Felicita. Everybody knew everybody. When a strange face walked in everybody stopped talking and turned round to see who'd just walked in. It must have been a bit unnerving for strangers sometimes.

One evening the place was buzzing with the usual suspects. A couple of English tourists had been in the bar for a while having a few drinks. They were getting drunk and rowdy and started making racist comments towards the Chinese, so it was time for them to leave. I went up to them at the bar and suggested that they pay their bar bill and leave without a fuss. They didn't like this idea and got a bit lippy so I told them if they didn't leave quietly then my Chinese friends would make sure they left in a body bag. They paid their bar bill and left without a fuss.

A few nights later I was in the bar. It was quiet, only Arif, Steve, Phil and Bernie were present. A stranger came into the bar and decided to sit himself down at the bar right next to me. The guys were sat a short distance away in the usual corner. For a while he sat there drinking a few beers in silence. Then he decided to engage me in conversation which revealed the fact that he was going to be a nuisance.

Bernie came over and quietly asked me if I was ok. I told him the guy was no problem. Unfortunately the guy was persistent and becoming a pain in the ass. I told him to leave but he wasn't having any of that. I was just about to ram my elbow into his right ear and drag him out of the bar. Suddenly Steve appeared behind the bar, sticking his face close up to this guys face he told the guy to fuck off before he got thrown out. The geezer quickly left, never to be seen again.

Many a crazy scheme or plan or dodgy deal was hatched in the Bar Felicita. One crazy scheme in particular involved stealing bicycles. The stealing of bicycles wasn't new in Amsterdam, it happened all the time. Often you would come across a junkie cycling round town trying to sell you a bicycle. Usually for between ten to twenty five guilders, depending on the quality of the bike and the desperation of the junkie. I often bought a bicycle for the sheer joy of buzzing off around town at four in the morning. Invariably the bicycle would end up being stolen again a few days later, sometimes by the same junkie.

I was in the bar one night drinking beers and smoking joints with Scottish Gerry, Steve and Phil when I put forward the suggestion that we start stealing bicycles. The boys were interested so I outlined my plan. I explained that every time one of the croupiers went back to England, instead of flying we convince them to go by ferry and take a bicycle with them. At the other end we would arrange for the bicycle to be picked up and put in storage until we had enough stock to put on the market.

Gerry pointed out that taking the bicycles over individually would be a long drawn out and expensive business. He suggested we steal the bicycles, store them in a warehouse in Holland then ship them to England en-masse. Phil reckoned he could find a corrupt shipping clerk to supply the necessary paperwork and Steve knew a friend back in England who would be able to take care of distribution.

We were ready to rock 'n' roll. We were ready to strip the streets of Holland of all bicycles. We envisaged making thousands of pounds out of our little venture and maybe branch out to supply the rest of Europe with an inexhaustible supply of stolen bicycles.

Of course it was just another dodgy scheme dreamt up over a few pints of beer and a few strong joints. The next day we were back doing what we did best. Dealing roulette and blackjack and making our bosses richer. The wild scheming of the night before long forgotten.

Phil was always finding new things to get into. He was the first to join a gun club. He was also the first to get involved in go-karting. One day a whole bunch of us went out to the track with him. We'd have a few beers then go out and do a few laps round the course and set up races. It was during one of these races when I did something that was supposed to be physically impossible in a go-kart. I actually flipped over whilst taking a corner at speed and rolled over about three times before coming to a stop against a bale of hay. I was unhurt. It was fun. Never managed to do it again. Phil was well into his karting and ended up buying his own go-kart. After a few months the excitement wore off, he sold his go-kart and moved on to another venture, buying diamonds.

Another of our more sensible ideas was hatched between Gerry, Phil and me. We thought it might be a good idea to buy ourselves a boat, as we were surrounded by water. After a discussion and a bit of research we ventured out of the city to a boatyard. We were going to buy ourselves a speedboat. Arriving at the boatyard we had a look around at what was for sale and we came across a very nice sleek looking red speedboat. It was in good nick and it had a good powerful engine. The boat yard owner was asking seven thousand guilders for it. The three of us retired to the local bar to discuss the buying of the boat. After a few beers we came to the decision not to buy the boat. We envisaged the three of us speeding around the canals one night drunk and stoned and wrapping the speedboat around one of the many bridges and killing ourselves. I suppose we could have gone for something less powerful but somehow that didn't seem to appeal to us.

Like riots, muggings were also common in the city. Goffie was mugged three times in one night, twice by the same person. When I was giving a tour to the new croupiers in town I would tell them to avoid the little alley ways at night and stick to the main streets. I was used to the alley ways and never had a problem until this one night when I stupidly got caught out.

I'd left O'Henry's and nipped round the corner to Steve's squat to deliver some money to him. After a couple of joints and a couple of beers I headed back to O'Henry's. Halfway down this alley way I noticed a couple of guys coming towards me. As they came up to me one of them asked me the time. I didn't look at my watch, I still had some street sense. I told them the time as I'd noticed it as I left Steve's. Next thing I know I had a small knife at my throat while his friend started going through my pockets. All I had on me was a twenty five guilder note in my pocket. But what they did get and what pissed me off was my gold plated lacquered Du Pont lighter.

For ten days after that I would go to O'Henry's after work, have a beer and in front of one of the croupiers I would empty my pockets out on the table. Picking up my knife and my can of C.S. gas I would go out hunting the alley ways hoping to find these two muggers and teach them a good hard lesson. After a few days of this the guys were getting curious as to what I was up to so I told them I'd been mugged and every night I was going out hunting for them. I never did see them again.

CHAPTER THIRTY THREE
RIOTS BEFORE CHRISTMAS

A new girl had joined us during the summer. She was an excellent croupier. Her name was Sara and she was from London. Five foot ten with a head of crazy brown frizzy hair and beautiful big brown eyes. We hit it off straight away. I was still doing a lot of cocaine which was making me dangerously crazy.

One afternoon one of the blackjack tables was doing its brains and I told Sara to go over and sort it out. She refused and she started to argue with me. If you're going to argue with me do it in private not in front of the staff and the punters. After work, down in Arif's I took her to one side and told her if she ever did that again I'd have her shot. Sara was a bit taken back at that but as soon as it began it was over and nothing was further said.

In the number 7 we had these two Indian Sikhs who used to come in and at every opportunity would try and cheat on the roulette tables. One of them had followed us to the number five. Every afternoon he would come in and without fail would always try and pull a fast one on the tables. It was as if he had an addiction for cheating. He wasn't even good at it, he always got caught.

One day he moved a few hundred guilders onto high numbers after the ball had dropped. I picked up his late bet and slammed it down on the table in front of him. I got myself taken off the table and I stormed into the office to see Big Chris. I told Chris I was fed up with this guy coming in every day and trying to cheat. I told Chris I was going home to pick up some money and I was going to see the Chinese about putting a contract out on the guy.

Big Chris told me I couldn't do that. I told him to give me a good enough reason. Chris told me that the guy was an Indian diplomat and it wouldn't look good to have Indian diplomats found floating in the canals. I calmed down and saw his point but told Chris to sort out the problem. He must have spoken to the guy because I never saw him in any of the city's casinos ever again.

The raiding season was upon us. Throughout the city and up and down the country casinos were being raided and shut down. The number 5 escaped the attentions of the police so it was business as usual. The police were especially busy at this time of the year. The local authorities had decided to clear out a block of flats that had been squatted for years.

Squatters didn't just pack their bags and leave, they put up a fight. Amsterdam was notorious for riots. Any excuse and the people took to the streets to vent their anger. Before I arrived in Amsterdam they had an enormous riot when city hall tried to evict hundreds of squatters in a large block of flats up by the Waterloo Plein.

I witnessed two riots whilst I was living in Amsterdam. The first was from a safe distance. The second was a bit closer. It had been going on for hours moving into different parts of the city. Now it had worked its way to Dam Plein. Hundreds of rioters in motorbike helmets and sunglasses carrying chains, pieces of wood and brandishing bricks ripped up from the streets faced hundreds of police kitted out in riot gear with truncheons backed up with horses, dogs and water cannon.

Living close to Dam Plein and being on the street it was inevitable I would come across pockets of rioters making their way into the square to reinforce the others. I skirted round them trying to avoid both rioters and police. As I was crossing the road near the church to head for the safety of the flat the police gave a mounted charge.

Before I knew it I had a large crowd of rioters running towards me closely followed by several mounted police. I had no choice but to run with the crowd. Fortunately or unfortunately they were going my way. With the sound of horse's hooves clattering on the road behind me I headed for the flat. I unlocked the door and slammed it shut behind me and climbed the three flights to our flat. I opened the windows and sat there watching the rioting taking place below. It was a jolly good show. As usual the police eventually won.

My twenty sixth birthday came and went in a haze of booze, cocaine and hash. We had a double celebration in the Bar Felicita. Julie and Alan had decided to call it a day and head back home to Scarborough. They'd saved enough money to buy and run a nursing home. The bar was packed that night with people coming and going and we all got truly smashed.

Christmas was a blur. For New Years Eve Bernie and I decided to take the car and drive to Scarborough to spend it with Alan and Julie. We took the ferry from the Hoek of Holland and sailed over to Harwich and drove north to party.

CHAPTER THIRTY FOUR
BACK HOME

Bernie and I arrived back in Amsterdam on the second of January. It was straight back to work for the both of us. All was normal, nothing had changed. I remember dealing on the blackjack table. It was the twenty eighth of January, instead of a loud Chinese kung fu movie on the television some of the punters were watching the launch of the Challenger space shuttle.

When the Challenger exploded in the sky everybody just stopped what they were doing and stared at the screen. The punters I was dealing blackjack to went over and stood behind the settee to watch as events unravelled from NASA. I closed the lid on my table and went to join them, as did all the others. No one was gambling, everyone was temporarily stunned. It was a subdued evening in the bar that night.

With the raiding season over and the prospect of spring and summer ahead of us all without getting busted we got on with business. New croupiers came into town. One of the new girls to join us was a girl called Karen. She was a tall girl with long silky brown hair and eyes to match. She was a big girl but not fat. More work for me to find them jobs and flats. When I asked new arrivals what they wanted to see in the city I always got the same reply. The boys wanted to check out the girls in the windows and the girls wanted to check out the sex shops.

So I could often be seen leading a small group of male and female croupiers around the sights of the Red Light district. On one of my early evening tours I looked across the canal at a group of rowdy English tourists. One of the lads was checking out one of the girls in the window. He took a step back and had another look. He took another step back, then another, then another. I got bored and walked on.

There was a sudden loud splash and I turned back to witness this English tourist coming out of the water and clawing at the side of the canal then sinking under the water again. On his second attempt his mates grabbed a hold of him and pulled him out. I shouted over to them that they should take him to hospital for a tetanus injection then continued my tour for the newbie's.

Bernie was a qualified mechanic and being from a Dutch family he had got himself a job with the Ford motor company. At the beginning of the summer he had an accident at work and a gear box fell onto his thumb. This put him out of action for the duration of the summer. When it came to my days off I would fill up his petrol tank and we would go exploring around the country sometimes crossing into Germany and Belgium.

On one of our trips we decided to go and see Golden Earring, a Dutch band, perform live on Zandvoort beach. When we finally found our way to the beach we were too late. They'd played an afternoon concert and had packed up and gone. The beach still had several hundred music fans milling about getting drunk and stoned. It was still a beautiful sunny day so we decided to hang out on the beach and watch the sunset. Bernie spotted a small mechanical digger lying abandoned further along the beach. He decided it would be fun to hotwire it and drive up and down the beach. Alas with all his mechanical skills he couldn't get it started so he gave up and we went back to sit on the car and watch the sun set.

Squatter Steve had got himself a flat on Nieuwe Tuinstraat and a black BMW which had been sat outside the flat for a couple of months. It needed re-tuning and a general looking over so as Bernie wasn't working he decided to check it out. After several hours working on Steve's car it was decided to give it a road test.

All three of us piled into the car with Bernie driving. We hit the nearest garage to re-fuel. With the fuel tank full we hit the autobahn. I was sat in the back with my head hanging out the window as Bernie put his foot down. With the force of the wind full in my face I pulled my head back in and checked the speedometer. No wonder it was getting too windy, Bernie had floored the accelerator and we were doing 200km an hour. I glanced at the fuel gauge and watched the needle actually moving as we burned up fuel much to Steve's horror.

With fuel burning up too quick for Steve's liking he suggested we pull over somewhere. Bernie pulled off the autobahn and we drove down a quiet country road with no one else in sight. We stopped the car and got out to stretch our legs. It was then that we noticed that the spoiler on the back of Steve's car had disappeared. We concluded that it must have just flown off as we were cruising down the autobahn. Steve was moaning about his fuel tank getting low and bits of his car missing.

We wandered round and soon discovered we had driven into a grave yard. The gravestones weren't stood up as expected but were laid down flat in groups of four or six neatly boxed in by short hedges. It was a peaceful place so we continued wandering and sat down on the bank of a canal and smoked a joint in the sunshine before climbing back into the car and with Steve driving we headed back to the city.

CHAPTER THIRTY FIVE
LOOK OUT IT'S THE CHINESE MAFIA

Guns were an everyday part of life in the circles that I moved in. I'm not saying everyone carried one, but there always seemed to be a few who were permanently tooled up and those that tooled up if and when they were working. The Chinese in particular were renowned for carrying. Their choice of weapon usually being the 9mm semi-automatic.

It was a 9mm that I ended up looking down the barrel of late one afternoon on a summer's day at the number 5. It had been a quiet afternoon, unusual for us as we were always busy from the time we opened up at two in the afternoon. Big Chris hadn't even bothered to turn up so it just left Wendy in charge. What made it even quieter was the lack of the regular Chinese punters who would be in everyday gambling their ill gotten gains.

Ordinarily I would have been across the road grabbing a beer but as it was quiet and the tables were dead I took over control of the inner doors while our Chinese doorman, Fang, operated the outside doors through a sliding panel over one of the windows with a conveniently placed mirror for sight and recognition. There was a steady trickle of people coming in and out. Nothing exciting was happening. It was going to be a long boring shift.

The doorbell went and I got the thumbs up to open the inner doors. Eight of the regular Chinese boys walked through the door. "Look out it's the Chinese mafia." I said in jest.

"Come away from the door Red and stand out of the way." Chinese Michael said. I gave him a questioning look and the look I got back told me was serious and something was up. Suddenly everything happened at once.

As I was standing by Wendy Wu, the bosses sister, Michael pulled his 9mm and fired a bullet into the ceiling. He soon got everyone's attention. Addressing the few punters in the room he told them all to go and stand in the corner by the television and behave themselves. He told them if anyone pulled a gun they would be shot.

As this was going on some of the boys produced four plastic bottles filled with petrol. They placed one on each of the roulette tables and on the two blackjack tables. While they were doing this a couple of the others reached into the roulette floats and removed the hundred guilder chips, putting them in their pockets.

Chinese Andrew had pulled out his gun and was waving it about in front of me and Wendy, talking to her in Chinese. It didn't particularly bother me that I had a gun pointed at me as we partied and drank together. I had no idea what was going down but thought it best to move out of the line of fire and check up on the rest of the staff, the majority that day being the girls. Four of them were across the room by the blackjack tables.

Slowly I walked across the floor to the blackjack tables. They were looking pale and nervous. They weren't used to having guns waved about in front of them. I told the girls to relax, that nothing would happen to them and they would be let out if things got a bit too hot, so to speak. They asked me to go and get their handbags which they kept under the roulette table.

Satisfied that they were ok I took another lonely walk across the casino. I retrieved their handbags and slung them over my shoulders. "Bring them over here then." One of the girls shouted across. "I don't think so girls, I've crossed that floor twice and I'm not going to do it again, you'll have to wait." I shouted back.

As I was wandering across the casino, which was in the hands of eight gun toting Chinese, Michael got on the phone and was talking to somebody in Dutch. After a bit of a heated conversation he put the phone down. He said something in Chinese. Immediately the bottles of petrol were picked up, the hundred guilder chips were put back on the roulette tables and they made an orderly exit.

I gave the girls their handbags back and followed Wendy Wu into the office. She told me the reason for the sudden hijacking of the casino. It turned out that the night before some of the boys were gambling and lost heavily. Our practise was to give our high rollers a 'katje' (taxi money) usually ten percent. Big Chris had insulted them by offering them a derisory amount. They threatened to come back the next day and shoot his legs from under him. Hence his absence that day.

Wendy decided we should get back to business and open the tables. I told her that wasn't a good idea as a shot had been fired and the police could be here at any time. I also pointed out that the girls were not fit to deal as they had been shaken up a wee bit. Wendy reluctantly agreed with me. She paid off the croupiers and we left the casino leaving Wendy behind to empty the boxes of cash and lock up for the rest of the day.

We went round the corner to the Bar Felicita for a drink. The Chinese boys had had the same idea. They were lined up along the wall having a drink. We walked in, acknowledged each other and I ordered a round of drinks. Double vodka's with orange for the girls and double whisky with beer chasers for the boys. "Who's paying for this lot?" Anya asked.

"They are." I said indicating the Chinese boys behind me. That night they paid for everything and we all got rip roaring drunk.

The next day, apart from some serious hangovers, all was normal and it was back to business. When I woke up that next morning I felt something heavy on my right wrist. On inspection it was a solid silver bracelet. I had no recollection of buying a bracelet the night before so when I saw Anja later that day she enlightened me. She told me that we were all very drunk the night before and I had admired Chinese Alan's silver bracelet and he had taken it off his wrist and put it on mine. When I saw Alan later that night I tried returning it to him but he said it was a gift and I should keep it.

CHAPTER THIRTY SIX
INTO THE CELLARS AND OVER THE ROOF

It was an early November's evening at the number 5. We'd had a good run for the last two years but the inevitable was bound to happen and it was happening right now. We were under siege by Amsterdam's finest who had come along to raid us. It was going to take them awhile to get in, they had two doors to get through.

We emptied the boxes and Big Chris grabbed the float and told us to follow him into the basement where the toilets were. We weren't sure where he was leading us. Neither were some of the customers, who followed us down. Big Chris produced some keys and unlocked a door in the corner which led into the cellars.

We followed him into a long narrow poorly lit tunnel which had little dark unused rooms leading off it. We started to climb and it got brighter until we came to a door which Big Chris opened. Now we knew where we were. The door we had come to was the entrance to a block of flats, a few doors up from the casino opposite a small bar. Everybody followed Big Chris as he stepped out of the door and crossed the alley way into the bar.

Phil and I thought this was a silly idea. The police had just seen all these people of different nationalities emerging from a door and entering a small bar, a bit of a give away. Phil and I hung back and when everybody had left we closed the door and climbed the stairs into a maze of flats. Phil was carrying a black bin bag full of one hundred guilder chips which Big Chris had given to him. He was also carrying a couple of five gram lumps of some fine Afghan hash.

We knocked on several doors but there was no answer. We got to thinking that the flats were empty so we started to try to see if any of the doors were open. Eventually a door opened as we heard loud Dutch voices and heavy boots coming up the stairs. We went through the door onto a fire escape. Quick thinking Phil had grabbed the key on the way out and as we heard the police getting closer he locked the door.

Phil threw the two lumps of hash into the gutter above our heads along with the key to the fire escape. We could only go forward now so we jumped down onto the flat roof below us. The building next door had recently been demolished so we knew where we were in comparison to the casino. I explained to Phil that we had to jump down onto the next roof then jump down into the demolished site then circle round to avoid the police cordon.

We had no choice so we both jumped the six feet down onto the next roof then ran across it to jump the next six feet down into the demolished site. The early evening light was playing tricks on me and it was a good job I stopped at the edge before jumping because we were facing a twenty five foot drop onto god knows what.

A quick scan of the immediate surroundings showed me these old iron bars sticking out the wall in the corner at four foot intervals. It was like a ladder from heaven. I climbed down first. Phil threw me the bag of hundred guilder chips. I dropped the bag which split on contact with the bricks at my feet. Phil climbed down and we picked up the chips, filling our pockets.

We quietly crept across the demolition site and peeked around the corner. The police still had the alleyway cordoned off so we emerged from the darkness as casually as we could into the Kalverstraat and walked away from them. When we got to the next alley way we swung a right and walked down this to the end and crossed the Nieuwezijds Voorburgwal. We walked to the bar across from the alley way facing the casino and entered. Our hands were dirty, our clothes were dusty and our pockets were bulging with hundred guilder chips. We ordered two beers and took a seat in the window to watch the fun and games. We were fugitives.

The police had either broken through the doors or been let in. Police were going in and coming out with customers and some members of staff. People were being questioned, some were carted off in handcuffs and others were released. All those who had 'escaped' into the bar across the alleyway had also been rounded up. Big Chris was handcuffed and under police guard. The rest of the unfortunate members of staff were handcuffed and bundled into the back of a police van to be taken to the nearest police station for questioning.

When all had quietened down Phil and I went back to the flat. We showered, put on some clean clothes, stashed the chips and went out to the inevitable party. We found the fortunate few and started celebrating waiting for the release of the others. They weren't held for long and easily found us and we all got drunk celebrating our freedom.

The next day we got up, breakfasted and went back to work. It was business as usual, as if nothing had ever happened. Big Chris was delighted to be re-united with his hundred guilder chips and we learnt of the doorman's night. Fang had hidden in one of the dark cellars and had evaded the police for several hours until they withdrew.

A few days later news came to us that three casinos had been raided at the same time. This was unprecedented and highly organised. The police only ever raided one casino a day. We learnt that the Amsterdam police had brought in forces and equipment from other city's in Holland and they meant business. When they hit another two casinos the following night everybody started getting a bit nervous. Especially when one of those casinos was the Mata Hari. We were told when the police raided the casino they threw all the tables out of the first floor window onto the street below. Then they got out some chainsaws and in front of everybody they reduced the tables to matchwood.

Croupiers who had been arrested told us about this giant warehouse on the outskirts of town where they were taken for processing. They told us that the walls were covered with photographs of the casinos in the city and they had mug shots of people coming and going from these casinos. A mass of captured casino equipment was lying about on the floor of the warehouse and the questioning was quite intense.

CHAPTER THIRTY SEVEN
UNDER SIEGE AGAIN

Two weeks later we were under siege again. Big Chris opened up our escape route again and several members of staff and a few customers went through. Most of the punters stayed behind in the casino, they knew they were trapped. As we approached the exit into the alleyway I hung back and let the customers leave. I checked the alley and noticed that again we were cordoned off. So as they went out I went up.

Naturally I went for the fire escape then remembered it was locked and the key was outside in the gutter along with Phil's hash. I tried several other doors but they were all locked. I was trapped. I thought it would be ok if I sat tight and out of the way but some punters also wishing to avoid the police came back into the building. I'd forgotten to secure the door and I could hear their excited voices coming up the stairs.

I took up position at the top of a small flight of stairs leading to an apartment and told the rest of the rabble to go deeper into the building and hide. I didn't want to be connected to them in anyway. I tried the door to the apartment, it was locked. I sat and took stock of the situation. Unless I was lucky I was going to get nicked. So I emptied my pockets and stashed my drugs, weapons and any other incriminating evidence that I didn't want to fall into the hands of the law in this giant flowerpot behind me. I kept my money, cigarettes, lighter, flat keys, hip flask and passport on me. I was also carrying a plastic shopping bag with me with a couple of books inside which I'd grabbed on the way out of the casino. I sat back and had a cigarette.

I'd just finished my cigarette when I heard them coming in their heavy boots. Two policemen appeared at the top of the stairs in front of me. They saw me, stopped and asked me who I was and what was I doing there. I'd had time to think. Arif lived round the corner on the Kalverstraat. I told them I was looking for my friends flat around the corner when suddenly I was surrounded by all these strange people running around and policemen all over the place.

They asked me what I was doing in this building. I told them that I'd had a few drinks, holding up my hip flask, and I'd come in here to avoid whatever trouble was going on as I didn't want to get involved. Not a bad effort, but they didn't believe me. They noticed the carrier bag at my feet and one of them went to grab it. I picked it up and swung it away from him. That's when they reached into their holsters and I ended up with two semi-automatic pistols pointing at me. Wisely I handed the bag over and they asked me for identification.

Slowly I reached into my pocket and handed over my passport. They took it, opened it, looked at me then one of them put it in his pocket, he told me to stay put and not go anywhere. Then they left me and went off to search the rest of the building. I took stock of the situation. It was Saturday night and I figured these guys were from the police station on the Warmoesstraat in the Red Light district. I didn't fancy being banged up there for the evening so I made a quick decision and decided to do a runner. I'd worry about my passport the next day.

I went down the stairs and poked my head outside the door. The police were still at the bottom of the alley but they had withdrawn from the top so I took my chance and casually walked up the alley away from them. When I crossed the Kalverstraat and went down the alley on the other side I broke into a run onto the Rokin where I happened to notice some heavily armed police on patrol. Wondering what the fuck was going on I didn't stop until I got to O'Henry's.

I ran into O'Henry's, parked my ass at the bar and ordered a beer and a double scotch and asked what was with all the armed police crawling all over the city. I was told that there were some high level dignitaries visiting the Queen at her palace in the 'Dam' round the corner from the casino. Later I met up with the rest of the crew and told them of my exploits that evening as we had another party.

The next day I went back to work only to find that the entrance to the casino had been bricked up. Boarded up, not a problem, but bricked up meant the police were serious and were sending a message. I didn't get nicked but I'd lost my job and my passport.

I went to the police station on the Warmoesstraat in search of my passport. I gave the desk sergeant the same bullshit story I'd told the policemen the night before but they didn't believe me either. They told me my passport had been forwarded to the police station on the Marnixstraat just along from the Leidse Plein. I told them I knew where it was and that I would go down and collect it. They told me it wouldn't be there for a couple of days as they'd put it in the post. Put it in the post, what the fuck was all that about? A police car could have delivered it in less than ten minutes.

A couple of days later I went down to Marnixstraat to collect my passport. I fed them my story again, which they didn't believe and confirmed they'd received my passport but had forwarded it by post to the police station on the Linnaeusstraat. A few days later I went along to my third police station. It would have been less hassle getting busted. I told them I needed my passport as I had to get back to England for a wedding. More bullshit but I thought it might hurry them along a bit with very few questions asked.

They believed that story because they told me they knew I had worked at the number 5 but as I was leaving the country they weren't bringing any charges against me. They returned my passport and gave me a green card to hand over to immigration when I left the country. I had a feeling this card was me being deported somehow so now I had to leave the country. Not leaving the country might catch up with me later.

Soon after the number 5 was closed down we learnt that Chinese Andrew had been sent down for seven years. He'd cut the throat of a Moroccan in the Red Light district. The story that reached us was that this particular Moroccan had bad mouthed Andrew in a busy casino in front of everybody. That was a bad move. When this Moroccan left the casino Andrew followed him out and cut his throat in front of all the tourists. The Moroccan obviously died and Andrew got seven years.

With Christmas only a week away and no sign of work coming our way Sara, Bernie and I along with Ken decided to go to England for the Christmas period. Bernie had been getting on well with Sara's sister, Angela, and wanted to spend Christmas with her. So all four of us caught the train down to the Hoek of Holland and boarded a ferry for home.

CHAPTER THIRTY EIGHT
1987

With Christmas over and New Years Eve behind us Sara, Bernie and I returned to Amsterdam. I moved into the flat with Sara, Sian and Steve on the Nieuwendijk. I'd found three large square cushions which were strung together. Piled up they formed a chair. Laid out flat they became my bed which I made up outside Sara and Sian's bedroom on the bottom floor. Sara found work somewhere. Through Phil I got a job working for his mate Patrick in Den Hague. I used to commute from Amsterdam with Cheryl. She was a few years older than me. Short strawberry blonde hair, blue eyes and a fondness for her Vodka. Needless to say we got on quite well.

After about a month of travelling between cities I managed to find work again in Amsterdam. I didn't like working in Den Hague. It felt like I was out of my comfort zone, totally alien country to me. I can't remember where I was working. Early 1987 is a blank page on my memory banks but life went on as usual through the rest of the winter, into spring and summer.

Sometime around July things were turning bad again so Sara and I decided to pack up and move back to England. We couldn't take everything with us in one go so we left stuff with Sian and Steve. I returned to Amsterdam in early August to pick up some more of our belongings.

Flying back into Heathrow airport was a bit embarrassing as customs decided they wanted to check my bags. Before opening one of the big suitcases I told this customs official that the contents inside belonged to my girl friend. He made quite a display of pulling out knickers, bras, stockings and high heeled shoes. I did plan a second trip to pick up more stuff but I learnt that Sian and Steve had left the flat and also returned to England. So anything we had left behind was lost.

CHAPTER THIRTY NINE
LOOSDRECHT

Living in London and working at the Park Tower casino had left me penniless so I borrowed a £1000 off my mother and in April of 1989 I returned to Amsterdam. After a bit of hanging about I managed to get a job back in the '88' where I first started in1981. Only this time I was working for Leo's nephew Jan, but I had to wait awhile until word came down from Theo that I could work there again. Jan had three other partners. One was Steve, the other two I can't remember their names. The casino was busy both day and night. They even opened upstairs and put in three more blackjack tables.

I got myself a flat and was soon back into the life of Amsterdam. After three months as promised I paid my mother back £1250. She wasn't expecting the added percentage but I told her that's the way I worked. Jan put me in charge of running the Pit. We had two American roulette tables and four blackjack tables with another three upstairs. The only downside was I also had to take orders from his three other partners telling me how to do things which really got up my nose.

After a few months Theo offered me a job in his casino out in the countryside in a place called Loosdrecht. As I'd worked for Theo before when he had the '88' and Jan was a nephew of Leo there was no problem of Theo poaching me from Jan. After all it was a family affair.

I would work the first four hours for Jan in the '88' then at ten o'clock Big Joop would drive me out to Loosdrecht to work an eight hour night shift. Sometimes we would drive out via the brothel that Theo and Erwin owned. It was run by Theo's brother and it was a classy joint. Big Joop dealt French roulette in one small room. There was a bar, a swimming pool and a sauna. The madam in charge showed me round the rooms. Out the back was a large well kept garden where they had barbecues in the summer and the girls were choice. Over the months I kept trying to convince Theo to install a blackjack table and let me be the house dealer. He wasn't having any of it. Kept telling me he had no space. I suggested he put the table in the corner by the swimming pool. It never happened.

On one occasion at the brothel Theo's brother told me to help myself to one of the girls, on the house. Not one to turn down such an offer I picked out this cute petite Spanish girl and we went off for me to have my wicked way. After about an hour and a half there was a frantic knocking at the door. It was Theo telling me to get dressed as I had to go to work. At the end of the shift Big Joop would drive me back to the '88' and I would deliver the nights winnings to Jan in the cash desk.

The casino in Loosdrecht was a detached house surrounded in its own grounds set back from the road. Theo and Erwin had a partner out there called Bart along with his younger wife, Astrid, who were old business partners of Leo. You entered through the front door into a small hall way which was used as the reception area. To the right was a large room with a built in bar which housed one American roulette table, a French roulette table and a blackjack table. Off from this room was a reasonably sized kitchen. There were other rooms in the house, including an upstairs but they weren't in use.

This was no casino catering to the sort of punters I was used to dealing too in Amsterdam. This was more upmarket, a better class of punter with serious money. Though having said that not all our high rollers were of a 'better class'. There was a regular group of guys from the Middle East who were in the 'catering trade' that would come in and drop obscene amounts of money on the blackjack table. They were an arrogant lot as well. They were getting a bit mouthy one night to me. Being used to speaking my mind in Amsterdam and getting away with it I came back to them with a retort which they didn't like. They threatened to kill me. Guess I'd upset their macho Middle Eastern sensibilities. Theo had me taken off the table and we went into the kitchen out of sight. He shouted at me nice and loud so they could hear him telling me to show a bit of respect then he slammed his palm down on the wooden work surface and winked at me. Lowering his voice he told me to keep my tongue under control and continue taking there money and to pretend that he'd slapped me one across the face in his 'anger'. I understood his point and cooled it with these guys. I came out of the kitchen looking sheepish and thoroughly told off and went to deal some American roulette out of their way.

After a few weeks of this I decided I couldn't run the Pit in the '88' for Jan when I wasn't there so I suggested he find another Pit Boss. Michelle was chosen, she happened to be having a thing with Jan's partner, Steve. I didn't think she was the best choice but at the end of the day it wasn't for me to say. When I would return from Loosdrecht at six in the morning, the '88' was open twenty four hours, I would check on the Pit and the figures for the night and would make changes where needed. This would piss Michelle off and she would complain to Steve.

I continued working for Theo and Erwin throughout the summer. One evening when it was quiet we were sat out on the veranda enjoying a balmy summers evening. All of a sudden a convoy of classic American cars drove by. They must have been to some rally during the day. For about fifteen minutes a string of bright shiny Cadillac's, Chevrolets, Oldsmobile's and other makes of American car drove past the front of the casino and disappeared into the night.

Later in the summer Theo poached Big Ron, this Dutch guy from the '88'. He could deal French roulette and Baccarat. Theo wanted him to help Big Joop and to work when Big Joop was on days off. Theo was getting a good crew together. Astrid's husband, Bart, passed away. Leaving the three of them in charge. We were making good money and to avoid paying any 'taxes' the guys decided to have a big party.

No expense was spared. The casino had a good clean. More tables were bought in. A marquee was erected out the back to accommodate the vast buffet laid on and flowers were arranged all round the casino. Theo borrowed waitresses and croupiers from the '88'. The guys wore hired evening suits with black bow ties and Cummerbunds and the girls were kitted out in evening frocks. Invites went out to all of the regular punters and a few V.I.P's. On the night we all met at the '88' and a convoy of staff were driven out to Loosdrecht.

It was the busiest night I'd seen at the casino. Everybody was on their best behaviour. The customers had made the effort and everybody was dressed in their smartest outfits. Even the 'Middle Eastern' boys made an effort. Theo had put me in charge of the blackjack and American roulette tables while Big Joop ran the French roulette table and Big Ron took care of the Baccarat table. Theo, Erwin and Astrid, also dressed in their best, circulated and played the genial hosts.

After a couple of hours I did a table check and we were doing our brains. Money was flowing across the tables but going the wrong way. At one stage my tables were doing fifty thousand guilders. Theo told me to keep a tight control on the table losses but didn't seem too perturbed about it. This after all was an exercise to avoid paying any taxes on profits over the year. The entertainment went down well, the buffet was a success and everybody enjoyed a night of serious gambling.

Eventually the evening petered out and we finally closed at about five thirty in the morning. While Theo, Erwin and Astrid went out back to empty the drop boxes the staff were left to devour the remains of the buffet and attack the bar. There were plenty of bottles of champagne left so we all grabbed a bottle each and we partied. With the count done Theo handed me the keys to the casino with instructions to clean up and lock up before I left. With the bosses gone we continued to party until about eight in the morning, the casino was secured and a convoy of drunken and stoned croupiers made their way back to Amsterdam. I got dropped off at the '88' and I delivered the keys to Jan and went home to get a good days sleep.

CHAPTER FORTY
LEAVING LOOSDRECHT

I continued putting in my hours at the '88' and working the nightshift at Loosdrecht. I was working twelve hours a day and travelling back and forth between Amsterdam and Loosdrecht. In between on days off I was still partying like a mad man and taking vast quantities of cocaine to keep me going.

I decided I couldn't go on like this so I had a word with Theo. I told him I would work for him but I wasn't going to die for him so we agreed I would leave Loosdrecht and concentrate my talents back in the '88'. Michelle was safely ensconced as the Pit Boss. It was agreed that she would run one shift and I would run the other.

Work was good, we were busy, and I was on a good earner. As far as I was concerned Jan was my boss and to hell with his partners. Which is where I came unstuck. One afternoon I collared Steve and told him I wanted to speak to the boss. He told me he was the boss and I could speak to him. I told him I wanted to speak to the real boss. Which didn't go down so well.

Later that day Jan turned up. I was busy dealing a heavy game of blackjack. Jan smiled at me as he walked by and entered the cash desk with Steve. I could see but I couldn't hear as Jan and Steve got into a heated argument. After a while Jan walked out of the cash desk looking agitated. One of the dealers came and took me off the table and told me Jan wanted to see me. I caught Jan's eye, he caught mine and motioned for me to meet him upstairs.

Upstairs was empty. We both sat down at one of the blackjack tables and that's where I learnt my fate. Jan liked me and respected me but because of my lack of respect to his partner Steve I had put him in a difficult position. Jan told me he had no choice but he had to fire me. He gave me three days wages and told me to leave the casino. I grabbed my coat and quietly left the '88' for a second time. Italian Tony followed me out. He couldn't believe what had happened. We went to a bar, grabbed a drink and he told me to go and see these guys who were operating in Frans Diggelen's old place down on the Weteringschans just off the Leidseplein.

I was in no hurry, I had six hundred guilders in my pocket. I went and scored some cocaine and a bag of hash and I went out and got drunk. For me getting fired was a rare occurrence.

CHAPTER FORTY ONE
WORKING FOR A DUTCH CREW

After a few days on the piss I realised I had to get back to work. So I went to see the people that Italian Tony had told me about. They were operating in Frans' old place the Hermes, just off the Leidse Plein. This was a casino I rarely visited in the previous years as it was a bit more upmarket compared to some of the other casinos in town. With Frans gone this place was just another casino.

The place was being operated by a Dutch crew of about six. I didn't know any of them so they must have been from out of town. They had set up in the basement where Frans used to operate from, and the place was crammed full of blackjack tables. I got myself a job, no problem, I was earning again.

We were busy. Just as busy as the '88' and there was a lot of us working there. Some of the old crew but a lot of new croupiers fresh off the boat. We worked hard and we partied hard. The one good thing about working for these guys was at the end of every shift they would supply us with a crate of Heinekens, and a bottle of vodka, brandy and whisky. So we just sat around getting drunk and stoned after work.

It was working in the old Hermes when I finally came across this legend called Big Dick. Peter 'the prat with the hat' had told me a story about him once. Peter was dealing blackjack in the '217' one day when Big Dick had come in with a friend of his. They were both wearing hats and long fur coats and Peter thought they were just a couple of gay guys. Big Dick was doing his brains and getting a bit agitated with him. As Peter pulled another ten Big Dick pulled out a gun and told Peter if he pulled an ace to go with the ten he would shoot him. Peter realised he had no reason not to believe him so he turned the shoe around and told Big Dick to pull the card. With a sneer Big Dick pulled the card and threw it down on the table. It was an ace, another blackjack for the house. Big Dick muttered something incomprehensible to Peter and walked away without shooting him. So this was Big Dick. A man not to be messed with. Known to shoot up casinos if he was losing. Luckily our paths didn't cross that much and when they did I never had a problem with him. Guess I was lucky.

Big Dick came in one night and did his brains. He wasn't a happy chappy and when we closed he was still on the premises. There was going to be a show down so when we all got paid we were told to leave immediately. I never found out what happened but it was business as usual the following night.

Our Pit Boss at the time was an English girl. I can't remember her name. I can't remember the names of most of the crew I worked with. I remember that Pete 'the prat with the hat' was one of them. One day our English Pit Boss left, don't know why, but she was gone. As usual I stepped in and took over running the place. I did this for about three or four nights then I approached one of the bosses to discuss running the Pit on a permanent basis.

He was happy for me to run the Pit. I was happy to run the Pit but when it came to discussing wages we had a problem. I was earning two hundred guilders a shift as a dealer. The going rate in the city for a Pit Boss was two hundred and fifty. I told him that is what I wanted to be paid. He said no. He told me the last Pit Boss was on the same money as everybody else. I told him she was a fool and demanded the going rate.

He wasn't having any of it. He told me to go downstairs and run the Pit for two hundred a shift or put my coat on and fuck off. So I went down stairs, put on my coat and fucked off. His face was a picture, he couldn't believe I was walking out on him, but I had my principles. Later in the bar I saw some of the other croupiers from the place. They told me I was mad as there wasn't a lot of work in town at the time. They were right, but I stuck to my guns. So here I was again, back on the street with no money and no job.

CHAPTER FORTY TWO
THE VICTOR VICTORIA CLUB

I was out of work for a couple of months. I had to give up my flat and ended up selling my silver Cartier lighter. Arif let me stay in his attic room. He fed me and kept me in beer at the bar. I'd get the occasional hand out from some of the working croupiers which kept me fed and in cigarettes. Joints would come my way and if I was really lucky the occasional line of cocaine. At closing time I would help Arif close up the bar. I would stack the bar stools on top of the bar and pick up the discarded ten and five cent coins which came with the packets of cigarettes from the vending machine. Arif and Anya's tip jar soon became full of IOU's from me as I struggled to survive.

Every day I would be out trawling the casinos, showing my face and hoping someone would give me a job. I was just about to pack it all in and borrow some money to fly back to England when I got lucky. Brendan caught up with me one night in one of the bars where I was bumming drinks and cigarettes and told me to go and see Martin at the Victor Victoria club on the Kerkstraat above the Homolulu.

I showered and shaved and made myself presentable and went to see Martin. Martin had been around for along time. He'd spent some time working for the Germans and he'd heard of my reputation so he gave me a job.

The Victor Victoria club used to be an exclusive night club. It was a small place with a Grand piano in one corner, a bar, four blackjack tables, one American roulette table and a room out back with a poker table. Martin was a nice chap, very easy going, but sometimes a bit strange. When we were on a losing streak he would reposition the tables in a different way. He called it Feng Shui. If that didn't work he placed cloves of garlic under the tables and sprinkled salt around the tables. He even went so far as to bring in a Surinam witch one afternoon when we weren't open who performed some weird ritual. I never got to hear about what went on that day.

Through Rudy, at the Village Hotel on the Kerkstraat next door to the Victor Victoria I got myself a room round the corner on the Leidsestraat. My new landlord was an old man, he'd known Rudy for years. He owned the property outright and he rented out rooms. My new abode was just that, a room. A double bed, a very large wardrobe, a chest of draws, a sink and a shower room in the corner. The toilet was communal. There was one feature that I liked. I could climb up out the window onto a secluded flat roof where I could sunbathe and read.

The Victor Victoria's fortunes were up and down. More down than up. One night Lange Marcel came in for a game of blackjack. He was doing his brains and running short of money. He needed a hundred guilders to double down on a hand. The only hundred he had left was a hundred guilder note that he had folded up into a 'wrap' to hold his cocaine. He pulled it out of his pocket and placed it on the table. It was still money so I took it. I told Lange Marcel that if he lost I'd also have the contents. He smiled at me and lost the bet. As he was getting up to leave I opened the 'wrap' to find it was empty. Lange Marcel smiled at me again and as he left I licked the last grains of cocaine off the note and dropped it down the box.

Our losing streak continued in the casino. One night Lange Marcel entered the premises and announced that Martin was gone and he was the new boss. Having worked for Lange Marcel before I was delighted. But Marcel had a partner with him. He was a Dutchman I'd never met before, a lot older than Lange Marcel and didn't seem to know much about the gambling business but he was o.k.

He had his fingers in other pies. One of which was money lending. He told me a story one day about this guy who owed him money and wasn't paying up so he put on his body armour, like chain mail, which he wore under his suit and went out and gave the guy a beating. He told me that it wasn't until the next day that he realised he'd forgotten that the poor guy in question had already paid up. That was my new boss.

He was only with us for a few months before he too was gone. Now Lange Marcel was the only one in charge and we could get down to the serious business of making money. Ronnie was still Lange Marcel's manager but Lange Marcel put me in charge of the Pit. He told me I could fire whoever I wanted and hire who ever I wanted. I told Lange Marcel I would make him a minimum of a hundred thousand guilders clear profit a month and set about trying to put a team of the best croupiers in town together.

I got rid of a few croupiers who in my mind weren't good enough and recruited some of the old school who at the time weren't working or wanted out of where they were. I couldn't get everyone I wanted. I wanted Brendan to come and join the team but he politely refused saying he had a good job with the Germans and he didn't want to burn any bridges. Which was understandable.

Wayan was our cashier. He was a short fat lovable gay Indonesian who had also worked for Lange Marcel before. On reception I had German Pete, a short but broad and very strong doorman who took care of any trouble. One of the croupiers that came my way was a beautiful blue eyed blond girl called Bettina who was married to an English croupier. Bettina was a great dealer, good for a laugh, intelligent and always up for going out for a drink or two.

Chinese Dave was also on the team. He was a brilliant blackjack dealer and knew the score. The 'score' being if you're winning, you stay on the table, if you're doing your brains, you take a break. He was half Dutch and half Chinese and was always stoned on hashish or grass. Chinese Dave rolled very strong joints. He'd buy a twenty five guilder bag of strong hash and put half of it in one joint. It blew your socks off, even for those who were experienced hash smokers. When the joints were being passed around you knew after just one hit you had just been given one of Dave's joints and you hurriedly passed it on or you'd be out of it for the rest of the evening. Often you would see someone passing a joint along warning them that is was 'one of Dave's'.

I had some other good croupiers on board but I also had a few weak ones who were soon replaced when someone better came along. At the end of the first month I went up to Lange Marcel and apologised to him. He asked me what I was apologising for. I told him I promised him a hundred grand profit a month but I could only give him ninety eight grand instead. He just smiled at me and told me to keep up the good work.

CHAPTER FORTY THREE
WHAT'S MY PERCENTAGE?

Business was booming. The money was pouring in, my win percentages on the tables were astronomically high. Tommy warned me that the percentages I was getting were very high and I was to expect some severe losses as in theory they should balance out to normal acceptable percentages of around eighteen to twenty percent.

One night when we closed Lange Marcel handed me the keys and told me I was opening up the next day. We opened at nine o'clock in the evening. I got there at quarter past eight, unlocked the front door and entered the casino. I turned on the lights, opened the cash desk and started to get the floats out for the roulette and blackjack tables. With the floats sorted I opened four decks of cards, checked them and spread them out across the blackjack table ready for a Chemmy shuffle. At eight thirty the door bell rang and I let in one of my dealers. I told him to cover the door while I finished sorting out the rest of the cards for the other blackjack tables.

Five minutes later the door bell rang again. "Red its Tony shall I let him in?" The croupier on the door shouted.
"Which Tony?" I shouted back.
"Tony from 'Fat City'." He replied. Tony owned a big hotel in the Red Light district called Fat City and was a good friend of Lange Marcel's.
"Let him in." I shouted back.

Tony came upstairs and asked if he could play some blackjack. Tony was a high roller so I wasn't going to say no. "Of course you can." I said. Leaving my dealer in charge of the door to let in the rest of the staff I shimmied the cards and a game of blackjack ensued. Four shoes later and thirty thousand guilders down the drop box Tony got up said thanks and left the casino. It was eight fifty-five.

As Tony was going through the door Lange Marcel rang and asked me if I was all set up to open. "I'm ready to rock 'n' roll and I'm already up thirty thousand guilders do you still want me to open?" I told him. Marcel asked me to explain so I told him what had just gone down. He was a happy chappy and told me to open as normal. I took the drop box out into the back room with Wayan and counted out the money and put it in the cash desk for safe keeping.

Big Dick was another high roller who used to come in and play at the Victor Victoria. Not only was he a dangerous gambler but he was also a dangerous man but as he was friends with Lange Marcel he never gave me any troubles. When he lost too much I would bung him a healthy katje and he would leave without a problem.

Everybody got a katje of ten percent if they lost a certain amount. Then one day in his wisdom Lange Marcel decided to cut the katje to five percent. When it came to a select few of our best punters I decided to stick to ten percent and argue the case with Lange Marcel at another time. One of those people was Big Dick.

When Big Dick came in next I took him aside and explained the situation. I told him he would get his ten percent but to be discreet about it. I told him if he lost I would come to him at the bar and slip him his money. We always kept a close tabs on what the punters were losing.

A couple of days later Big Dick came in and promptly dropped two thousand guilders. A paltry small amount for him so I went into the cash desk and Wayan gave me two hundred guilders which I slipped to Big Dick at the bar. Big Dick was in a bit of a dangerous mood that day and demanded another two hundred guilders. I said no. He insisted. Neither of us was going to budge. I couldn't be seen to lose face and Big Dick was just used to getting what he wanted.

I eventually managed to get him out on reception away from everyone else. German Pete was on duty that night. Him and Big Dick were good friends, thank God. Big Dick told me to give him an extra two hundred guilders so he could give it to German Pete as a tip. This seemed a good solution to the problem so I went back into the cash desk and told Wayan to give me another two hundred. I gave Big Dick his two hundred who promptly handed it over the German Pete then he left the building. German Pete just stood there with the two notes in his hand and looked at me as if to say 'what do I do with this.' I told him to put it in his pocket. When Lange Marcel came in later I told him what went down. He just looked at me and smiled and left it at that.

My percentages remained high. One night after closing we opened the boxes and counted the money. We had a drop of seventy five thousand guilders. I was looking at a win of seventy thousand. This was good, too good to be true and I was keen to know what my percentage was. For the life of me I'd forgotten how to work it out so I had four or five of my dealers sat at the bar having a drink and trying to work it out on paper. We couldn't find the calculator.

I know I can hear all you croupiers out there wondering how the hell a bunch of experienced croupiers in Amsterdam couldn't work out the night's percentage. It just seemed to be one of those nights when everybody's brains went to mush. Eventually Bettina, beautiful clever girl that she was came up with a figure. A ninety three percent win. My best ever and never realised since except for the time I took thirty grand off Tony before I'd even opened up. Lange Marcel was happy and we all went for a good drink that morning. Our end of month bonuses were going to be good.

CHAPTER FORTY FOUR
MY GUN CARRIES SIX

I had this one English croupier working for me. She was young and cute with a shock of long ginger hair. She may have been good to look at but she wasn't the best dealer I had. I wasn't responsible for employing her. One night one of the blackjack tables was doing its brains so I took her to one side and gave her some instructions on what to do. She went on the table and did the opposite to what I told her and consequently did her brains.

Later that evening when we closed I took her aside and had words with her. I told her to buck her ideas up and do what she was told to do. When she walked away from me she made the fatal mistake of back chatting me in front of the rest of the crew. So that was it, I told her she was a useless ginger twat and that she was fired. She went running off to Ronnie to appeal to his better nature, but that didn't work and she was gone.

Another night Chinese Dave was dealing blackjack. He was doing his brains, which was unusual. He kept on in the belief he could turn things around but it wasn't working. When he was busy shuffling I went up next to him and asked him why he was doing his brains. He told me he hadn't smoked a joint and was dealing straight. I couldn't believe it. Dave dealing straight was a first so I had him taken off the table and told him to go out back on the roof, watch the shooting stars and get stoned and to stay there until he was needed.

About a week later this guy came into the casino. He'd been in the previous two nights. Each time he seemed to be off his trolley on something. I don't think it was booze. On both visits I noted that he didn't drop much cash across the tables. What I did notice was his persistent pestering and sleazy comments he was making towards my female staff. This third night after half an hour I decided enough was enough. I bent down and whispered in his ear "I've had enough of you, cash in your chips, leave the casino and don't come back." He could have gone quietly but he decided against it.

"You can't throw me out." He shouted back at me.

"Yes I can, so cash in and go quietly." I said calmly.

"I'm not going anywhere, you don't know who I am." He said. Lifting his T-shirt to expose his chest he said "Look I've been shot five times, you can't throw me out." Looking at his chest I noticed what looked like five healed bullet wounds.

"Look mister." I was losing my patience now. "My gun carries six so if you don't fuck off I'll complete the set for you." As I said this to him I looked up and caught the eye of German Pete. He'd heard the shouting and come into the room. On catching my eye he leapt into sudden action. Picking the guy up in a bear hug he lifted him up from the blackjack table and hauled him out of the room and to the top of the stairs. I thought Pete was going to throw him down the stairs but he gave the guy a choice and he walked down the stairs.

Halfway down the stairs he turned back and looked at me. I thought here we go again. "If I see you on the street I'm going to get you." He said, and then he was gone. Three days later I saw him walking towards me on the Leidsestraat. He looked up and saw me. He crossed to the other side of the street and was never seen again.

CHAPTER FORTY FIVE
BACK TO THE 217

I had a Dutch couple working with me in the Victor Victoria. They were living in the city but also had a spare ground floor flat in the north of Amsterdam across the river Ij. It consisted of a living room, small kitchen and toilet with a back room which doubled up as the bedroom with a shower built in the corner. Upstairs was a very small box room and out the back was a small over grown garden. It was furnished with all the necessary amenities and the rent was acceptable, so I took it.

I gave my landlord on the Leidsestraat one months notice and began moving my stuff into my new flat. I had to get to the flat via a ferry service which ran from behind the railway station where a lot of the junkies and hookers hung out but they never gave me any problems.

I was seeing a lot of my old mate Gary who was now living with Karen on the Geuzenkade. Karen was going out with Orestos who was part owner of a Greek restaurant on the De Clercqstraat. Along with Tracey, Julie and Lorraine we took to hanging out at a new bar up the road from the Corner House. I can't remember the name of it but they sold Champagne cocktails which the girls were well into. It was at this bar that I got to meet Lorraine's husband, John and his partner in crime Kevin.

Kevin was an English man with long hair. A typical hippy looking like character. He designed and made jewellery some of which he wore on his waistcoat. Kevin had a darker side to him. He and John were drug smugglers. They did a lot of their business in Switzerland.

John on the other hand was a tough looking hombre with shoulder length hair and chiselled features. He was of Irish descent and sure as hell looked like he could take care of himself. I liked Kevin but I hit it off with John straight away and we started hanging out a lot together. John and Lorraine had an apartment down a small alleyway just off the Kalverstraat. I would often be there hanging out with John getting stoned, drinking beers and John would show me his knife collection. John was always giving me drugs, hash, grass, coke and ecstasy. He just seemed to have an unlimited supply around the flat.

One night hanging out at the champagne bar John came in and informed us that Kevin had been busted in Switzerland. He'd been caught with a shipment of drugs along with several hand guns and a pump action shotgun. He later got seven years. John was lucky to escape the same fate. He should have been there with Kevin but the night before he'd had a serious argument with Lorraine and decided to stay home.

Lorraine was heavily pregnant at the time with her first son. It was St Patrick's Day and with John being part Irish we were out on the town. The three of us went to an Irish bar on the outskirts of the Red Light district. It was a republican bar but as I'd been here several times before with John I was accepted. It did get a bit nervy when later on the Irish in the bar started singing republican songs. John made his excuses and left saying he had to do some business. I was left to take care of

Lorraine surrounded by all these jolly I.R.A. sympathisers. About an hour passed and there was no sign of John so we left the bar and got a taxi to another Irish bar down on the Rokin.

This bar was a nationalist bar and it was packed. Lorraine and I walked through the bar looking for John. There was no sign of him so we decided to go back to the other bar thinking he'd turn up there. Like I said this place was packed. It was full of great big fat hairy bearded men also singing songs. So with Lorraine in front of me I was shouting at these guys to move their asses as a pregnant lady was coming through. Like the Red Sea they parted and we got out of there. Outside looking for a taxi Lorraine said I didn't need to have done that. I told her maybe not but it was fun to watch all those burly Irish men move the way they did. Eventually John turned up as expected at the other bar and we continued partying through the night.

At around this time I came across a book called The Mafia in Amsterdam written by Bert Middelburg, published in 1988. I picked it up and had a flick through. It was written in Dutch and my command of reading Dutch was pretty poor. I had a look through the index at some of the names and I thought 'I know him, I've heard of him, I've worked for him and I work for him' I was sold so I bought the book. It was tough going trying to translate the parts that interested me.

Lange Marcel closed down the Victor Victoria club and we moved to the '217'. Working back at the '217' was good. We had one American roulette table and four blackjack tables with a full size Baccarat table down at the end. I was on the night shift one night and it was pretty quiet. This guy came in, one of our regulars and he wanted to play some roulette so I went over and opened the table for him. He threw me some money which got him a full set of colour, two hundred chips in total. He proceeded to plaster the layout mainly concentrating on the middle column. I went to spin the ball but he stopped me and threw me some more money so I gave him another set of colour chips. He did this another three times, each time adding to his bets on the middle column. This was unusual but I thought 'what the fuck, he's the only one playing'. When he was satisfied I span the ball and hit a number on one of the outside columns. Already he was on a loser. He'd given me all his money so he could only play with the chips he had left. After a few more spins he lost everything and left. Lange Marcel had been watching me and afterwards asked me why I'd allowed him to do that. I told him the odds were in our favour. His one column to our two. He saw my point and nothing further was said.

A few nights later Lange Marcel hosted a high stakes game of Punto Banco on the Baccarat table. The atmosphere was highly charged that night as some major players from all over Holland descended on the '217' to play. Each player bought a bodyguard and they all stood behind their respective bosses, every one of them was carrying the latest new gadget to hit the market. Each and every one of them was carrying the new mobile phones. As big as breeze blocks they were. That's the phones not the bodyguards.

At the time Lange Marcel was going out with Linda, one of the Indonesian croupiers. She had a lot of sisters and a few of them were working at the casino. We were working a busy day shift and Lange Marcel rang up to speak to Linda. He told her that he was in a high stakes game of poker and that he was winning three million guilders. He told Linda to take the day shift out for a meal and a piss up after work and put everything on his bill. So she did and we all had a great time. The poker game went on for another three days and when we saw Lange Marcel next he told us he'd ended up winning one and a half million guilders.

Ben my Egyptian poker dealing friend walked in one afternoon. We weren't busy but we still had quite a few punters in, mostly playing Kalooki on the card tables. I was dealing a quiet game of blackjack at the time and as he entered the casino he just stopped, looked around and in a loud voice said "fucking hell, I've never seen so many niggers in one room" then he just continued walking. Everybody looked up at Ben then just ignored him. I didn't know where to put my face. I was thinking 'how the fuck can he get away with that' but he did. Nobody said anything.

This guy called Kit appeared on the scene around this time. He was a big fat very loud Surinam who'd come up with a new angle for the illegal lottery. Just off the Dam Plein was an enormous pawnshop and once a week Kit would go along and purchase an item of jewellery. A gold chain, a gold ring or bracelet or a brooch encrusted with diamonds or other precious stones. The price of the lottery ticket depended on the price of the jewellery bought by Kit. The lottery ticket was only one number and that winning number was based on the bonus number drawn every Saturday night in the legal lottery. If you'd picked that number you won that article of jewellery. That's why the price of the ticket was different every week as only fifty nine tickets could be sold and not duplicated.

We were busy and we were making money and things were looking good. As November approached I realised that I was coming up for my thirtieth birthday. I wanted to do something special and decided to take a week off and travel to Berlin to see the 'Berlin Wall'. As things turned out it never happened. Which turned out to be very disappointing because on November the ninth the 'Wall' was torn down. I ended up watching it on the Dutch news thinking 'shit I should have been there'. Talk about missing out. Gary was in Berlin that night. He missed it as well, as he was in East Berlin having a meeting with some journalist friends of his.

I can't remember much about my thirtieth birthday. No doubt it was just another haze of drugs and booze. Christmas of 1989 was spent at Gary and Karen's flat on the Geuzenkade along with Orestos and Tracey. John and Lorraine were invited at the last minute and a good Christmas was had by all.

On New Years Eve Lang Marcel closed the casino early. I went home to change and eat and later met up with the gang at the champagne bar at about eleven fifteen p.m. Apart from me there was Gary, Karen, Orestos, Tracey, Julie and Brendan and John and Lorraine. We ordered a couple of pots of tea and sat there waiting for midnight.

We didn't drink much before midnight. We didn't see the point the bars never closed on New Years Eve so we decided to pace ourselves.

Just before midnight we ordered several bottles of champagne and went out on the street to witness all the fireworks going off. Nearly every year there would be at least five big firecrackers going off at the same time at midnight throughout the city. These giant fireworks would be hung across the streets and they consisted of about fifty thousand firecrackers which would explode for about thirty minutes. No matter where you were in the city you could always hear them going off. With the city like Beirut on a bad night joints were lit and one by one we payed a visit to the toilets to partake in lines of cocaine.

As usual I ended up doing a tour of all the local bars I often frequented. I would order drinks and buy drinks for everybody then I would wander off to another bar leaving my bar bill to be paid the next day on New Years day. At one stage during the evening I fell asleep at the bar in 'In the Mood'. No one disturbed me, they let me sleep. About half an hour later I woke up, ordered another drink and wandered off with glass in hand.

The next day I visited all the bars and paid off my bar bills. Nineteen eighty nine had been a roller coaster ride of a year. It turned out good in the end and now I was looking at nineteen ninety still stoned and wired and nursing a mild hangover. The night before I had managed to talk Lange Marcel into opening the casino at four o'clock in the afternoon instead of two o'clock. He agreed as long as I was the one to open up for him. So at three thirty with keys in hand I floated into the 217 and got everything all set up for another day of business.

CHAPTER FORTY SIX
WENT RIGHT INSTEAD OF LEFT

Nineteen ninety, a new decade and back in the 217. Lang Marcel had a new partner called Joop. A nice chap, I think he had a record shop on the Zeedijk behind the Red Light district. That was one street which I rarely visited as it was a well known hang out for the junkies. We were open both day and night so our staffing levels increased dramatically. We had a good team working there. Apart from most of the crew from the Victor Victoria we had Brendan, Justin and his wife Amy, Kenny, Hank, Chris aka Sooty and a new lad in town called Nobby. A big lad, must have been only about nineteen or twenty.

Ronnie was still Lange Marcel's katvanger. We had three brothers on the door, they were Jerome, Chris and Robbie. Robbie was o.k. Jerome was slightly deranged and Chris used to use me as a dumbbell. He'd pick me up straight off the ground, throw me over his head and bench press me half a dozen times. Good lads to have around if we had any trouble. They were three of seven brothers. The elder of the three I never met but he was reputed to be really scary. One night when I was out on the piss the usual Chinese boys entered the '217'. They'd had a few themselves and were messing about and Chinese Allan pulled his 9mm semi-automatic out, stuck it out the window and put a round into the roof of a car. The car belonged to the elder brother and as you can guess he wasn't too happy about this. The next night Jerome phoned his brother to tell him the Chinese were back in the casino so he decided to pay them a visit. Expecting trouble he came tooled up with a sub-machine gun. Needless to say he got an instant apology and a wad of cash to pay for the damage to his car.

A friend of Lange Marcel's also used to hang out a lot at the time. His name was Martin aka Lou. Martin liked a good joint so we got on well. I remember we were driving through the city at speed one afternoon when Martin asked me if I fancied a joint. I said yes and suddenly he did a three hundred and sixty degree handbrake turn in the middle of this busy intersection with trams, buses, taxis, bicycles and cars all around us and we took off down another street where he knew there was an excellent coffee shop. I was a bit shaken up by the sudden manoeuvre but I thoroughly enjoyed it. It was then that I learnt that Martins expertise was as a get away driver.

Recently a new bar had been opened by some English guys on the edge of the Red Light district. I can't remember the name of it or the owners, though years later Jerry Callaghan told me he was one of them. The bar opened in the early hours of the morning and they did an excellent English breakfast so of course it was a hit with all the English croupiers in town.

One Sunday morning after a busy night shift I was in there. I'd just finished a plate full of eggs, sausages, bacon, beans, tomatoes and toast and was washing it all down with a couple of cold beers and some whisky chasers. The bar was busy as usual, packed with croupiers, hookers, drug dealers and punters.

I'd recently learnt a new trick for taking cocaine. Empty out the end of a cigarette, pour in some finely ground cocaine, light the cigarette and inhale deeply, instant hit. So this particular morning I thought I'd give it a try and as usual I went over the top. I emptied half the cigarette, packed it full of coke and lit up. A strong smelling cloud of burning cocaine wafted down the bar. The customers at the bar all breathed in deeply. The staff behind the bar gave me daggers and requested that I don't do that again. Smoking dope was o.k. but the coke should be done discreetly in the toilets.

I was stoned, drunk and definitely wired. The sun was on the way up so I decided to leave and head for home across the river. I'd done this journey many a time in this state. Usually I just went into auto pilot and always managed to wake up at home. This particular morning, for some strange reason, I turned right instead of left and I started walking.

I was walking for a long time before it dawned on me that there was nobody around. No people, no cars, no taxis, no trams. I stopped and looked around. Where the fuck was I? The roads were deserted and instead of houses and shops and bars all I could see were warehouses. I prided myself on knowing the centre of Amsterdam like the back of my hand but I had to admit I was totally lost.

I had two choices, keep going until I came to a familiar landmark like a building or a canal or re-trace my footsteps. If I kept going I could end up on the wrong side of town so I turned around and tried to remember where I had just come from. Eventually after what seemed like ages I arrived back outside the English bar. The sun was high in the sky and burning into my cocaine addled eyeballs. Once I knew where I was it was easy for me to get back home. I made it in one piece and had a good days sleep. After that I was always careful about taking the right route home.

CHAPTER FORTY SEVEN
EIGHT NOTCHES ON HER GUN

I was working on the day shift and it was very quiet. Just a few sad bastards with nothing better to do than hang out in the casino playing Kalooki or Russian Poker. I've dealt roulette and blackjack to many people over the years and I never knew their names. As long as they behaved themselves and lost their money I wasn't interested in who they were or what they did.

One woman in particular would come in every day and play blackjack for hours on end. Like me she was not great at conversation. She must have been in her early to middle sixties and was no beauty. She was just plain miserable. I said something to Hank about how miserable she always seemed to be. Hank told me she used to own a revolver with eight notches on the barrel. I asked him to explain and he told me she used to be in the resistance during the war. I never did learn her name but she got my respect after that.

It was around this time that I decided to join a gun club. Phil had been a member since we lived together on the Nieuwezijds Voorburgwal. He hadn't been there long when our flat had a visit from the police. It wasn't a full on raid they were just checking the flat because the gun club had reported a gun missing and Phil had been there the night before. Needless to say they didn't find anything. They even missed the ounce of heroin I had stashed in the wardrobe. So it wasn't that good a search.

Being surrounded for all those years by gun carrying villains I finally decided it was about time I learnt how to shoot a gun. So on the twenty-fifth of May I went to the 'Shogun' gun club on the De Ruiterkade behind the railway station. Phil signed me in as his guest and I signed up for membership. All I had to do was show some identification, supply an address and a photograph and I was accepted as a member.

I was introduced to a guy called Johan who was one of the guys in the club designated to teach new members the club rules and how to shoot. I was started of on the Smith&Wesson .22. A lightweight gun shooting small bullets, but just as deadly. One of the weapons of choice used by the Mafia. Johan taught me how to hold the gun, how to hold myself, how to control my breathing and most important of all squeeze, don't pull on that trigger. When Johan was satisfied that I was safe and wasn't going to cause any fatal accidents he would leave me to it. I would pop off a hundred rounds a time getting used to the .22. It wasn't long before I was getting good regular patterns in the bull's eye of the paper targets we used.

Soon after joining the gun club I went out and bought an air pistol. I got it so I could practise my breathing at home and to get my grip right. I had a little metal target hooked up in the corner of the room, which caught the pellets instead of them lying about on the floor.

I soon found another target to practise on. I didn't like spiders and I wouldn't have them in the flat, so I used them as target practise. At first the pellets would be bouncing off the walls while the spiders would be scampering about trying to avoid these missiles coming their way. In the end I got good at taking out a spider in one shot at a range of fifteen feet. So I guess my practise paid off.

I got to become a regular. Shooting on days off, before shifts and after shifts when appropriate. I'd pop off fifty to a hundred rounds then sit at the bar having a drink and a chat with the regulars. At the end of the month Hank, one of the other tutors would gather all the club guns together, break them down and give them a good clean. I really should have paid more attention to his little monthly ritual and learnt more than just shooting them.

Eventually I got bored with the .22's and decided to move onto the .38's. Johan briefed me on the two .38's they had and the difference in ammunition used. They had a four-inch Smith&Wesson six shot revolver and a six-inch Smith&Wesson six shot revolver. After plenty of practise with both weapons I settled on the four-inch as my weapon of choice. It felt good in my hand and I was a lot more accurate with the four-inch as opposed to the six-inch. After a good session on the range I would take my targets into work and show some of the boys who also shot. Sometimes the punters would comment on my accuracy and I would tell them I was thinking of them at the time. Which got me some funny looks.

Visiting the club one night I noticed that Johan was on the range on his own. Several of the regulars were sat at the bar having a drink and observing Johan through the window behind the bar so I joined them. Johan seemed to take his time loading the gun. He took his time aiming and when he did squeeze the trigger about three feet of flame shot out from the barrel and a great cloud of black smoke fill the room.

I was intrigued so I went in to investigate. Johan was shooting a late nineteenth century Smith & Wesson navy colt .38 revolver. To load the gun you put the bullet in the chamber first followed by a sprinkle of black gunpowder then a small detonator. This was the reason for Johan taking a long time to reload. It also explained the great cloud of black smoke. I also noticed that Johan had rolled the carpet away from him for about four feet. I guessed that was down to the three feet of flame coming out of the barrel.

Johan offered me a shot, which I wasn't going to decline. I slipped the small solid round into the chamber, tapped in some gunpowder, inserted the detonator and took aim at the target twenty feet away. I squeezed the trigger. It seemed like a couple of seconds before anything happened. The navy colt had some serious kick back as it jerked in my hand. A long yellow flame followed a big bang. I missed the target and got a face full of black smoke and powder. Well worth the experience.

From the .38 I moved onto the 9 millimetre semi-automatic and the .357 Magnum revolver. The .357 was a nice gun. Comfortable in the hand, nice weight, hell of a kick back but accurate with practice. Hank owned a nice .357 Magnum revolver and he taught me how to shoot it. When I could I would keep in practice with it. My favourite though was the 9mm Browning semi-automatic with the fourteen shot magazine.

Good weight, good balance, accurate and with fourteen rounds in the magazine and one up the spout a hell of a lot of firepower.

There was one regular member who would come in and practise all night with his own Colt .45 semi-automatic. He would take such a long time lining up his shot but his every shot was a bulls' eye. I never knew his name. Never approached him, he seemed distant and in his own world. It was probably a good thing not knowing him as it turned out he was a police officer.

I was on the range one night with Johan and Hank. We were all firing away doing our own thing when suddenly my target exploded and disintegrated. I stopped shooting and asked the guys what the hell happened. It was common practice for these two jokers to let off a couple of rounds at someone else's target as a joke but the targets never disintegrated like that before. In this instance it was Johan who was responsible. He showed me the latest bullet he'd made. Johan had a special licence to make most of the bullets used on the range and occasionally he would play and come up with something special. His special that night was exploding bullets. He'd got hold of some hollow point ammunition and filled the end with an explosive mixture and sealed it with wax. On contact the bullet would explode, not exactly legal. He had a few rounds with him so I had a go.

One night I bought John to the club. I knew he was proficient with firearms and I thought it good to get him out the house for a couple of hour's relaxation on the range. I introduced him and he was signed up as a member. He suggested we keep his proficiency with firearms quiet and he would pretend to be a beginner. I was expecting Johan or Hank to take him on the range and teach him the basics but instead Johan turned round and said I was good enough and sensible enough to do the job. So we both picked out a .22 each and a couple of hundred rounds of ammunition and I went through the motions of showing John the ropes. Before long he to was a regular and we would pop off hundreds of rounds of .38's, 9mm's and .357's.

On some nights there would be Brendan, John, Phil and myself on the range blasting away for hours on end before going out to get drunk and stoned and wired. A great way to relax and unwind and take out any pent up aggression. After twelve months membership at the club I was eligible to apply for my very own gun licence. Which meant I could go out and buy my own gun. But as I was illegal and not registered as living in the country I wasn't able to do that. In nineteen ninety one the club closed down and I never got to go shooting again.

CHAPTER FORTY EIGHT
VINCENT VAN GOGH HEIST

John and I were chilling out in a bar waiting for the gun club to open. I picked up a recent copy of Time magazine from a table and had a flick through. I came across an article about Vincent Van Gogh. Holland was planning to celebrate the centenary of Vincent's death and they were planning to do it in style.

On the twenty ninth of July they planned to exhibit all of Vincent's work in a large art gallery somewhere in the south of Holland. Works of art were being shipped in and flown in from around the world. Vincent's paintings, drawings and etchings which resided in the Vincent Van Gogh museum in Amsterdam were to be transported by road in a large convoy two days before the exhibition. An idea was forming in my head. I finished reading the article and told John all about the convoy of priceless works of art. I told him that while they were on the road they were more vulnerable to a heist than if they were secured in a gallery.

John liked the idea of a major art heist. But being a practical man he pointed out we only had eight days to plan the job. We needed more bodies, transport, firearms, communications, a helicopter for aerial surveillance, an escape route, a hiding place for all those valuable works of art and more importantly a connection to fence the stolen artwork.

John also pointed out that such an audacious raid if successful would get worldwide publicity, attract too much attention from international law enforcement and make the paintings too hot to handle. He was right of course, nice idea but more advanced notice and better planning would be required next time such an opportunity came our way. Hanging out with John and going to the gun club on a regular basis maybe wasn't such a good idea. But what the fuck it was fun. From planning to steal thousands of bicycles and shipping them to England I was now planning a major art robbery. Never did get to see the exhibition.

John's son Charlie was about one year old by now and John and Lorraine really needed a good night out together so one night I volunteered to baby sit for them. With those two out for a night of debauchery I sat back watching some TV, smoking a joint and drinking some beers. Charlie was tucked up in bed. During the early hours of the morning Charlie woke up crying. I went to attend to him and found out he needed his nappy changing. Kids no longer wore nappy's in those days they wore pampers. Lorraine had told me where they were kept. So I took him into the bathroom and cleaned him up. I'd looked after kids many times back in England but I'd never put on a pamper before so it took me awhile to work out how they worked.

Job done we both fell asleep. John and Lorraine came home in the early hours of the morning to find me flat on my back in the middle of the floor fast asleep with Charlie fast asleep on top of me. The next day Lorraine thanked me for taking care of Charlie so well and pointed out that I had put the pamper on backwards.

CHAPTER FORTY NINE
DURING THE WAR

On the second of August 1990 Saddam Hussein invaded Kuwait. Living on the Jasmynstraat in the north of Amsterdam in an area heavily populated by Muslims Saddam's call for all Muslims to rise up in a Jihad was a bit worrying.

Day and night on television everybody watched the steady build up of coalition forces arriving in Saudi Arabia. Tension was building world wide as alliances were made and the Americans did their best to stop Israel going over the top. Meanwhile in Amsterdam, like 1982 when the British went to war with Argentina and we would often eat in the Argentinean restaurants there was peace. Everything went on as normal.

I say everything went on as normal but with Saddam stirring up the Muslims worldwide I decided to take precautionary action. I went to see John and told him I wanted to purchase a gun, preferably a semi-automatic with stopping power. A few days later I was round at John's flat and he took me into his bedroom where he produced a Colt .45 semi-automatic with its serial number filed off. It was a bit pricey and I would have preferred a 9mm but I didn't specify what calibre and I did say I wanted something with a bit of stopping power. A Colt .45 certainly had stopping power. It came with two clips fully loaded and as soon as I felt it in my hand and worked the action a couple of times I was sold.

When I got it home I sat down and gave the gun, the two clips and all the bullets a good wipe down, especially the bullets. Unlike a revolver which retains its spent cartridges in the cylinder an automatic ejects its spent cartridges and you don't want your fingerprints left lying around at the scene if you have to use your gun.

The only time I carried my gun was when I took it back to John's for him to show me how to break it down and clean it and how to clear any blockages. That was another problem with semi-automatics they tend to jam at the wrong moment. Carrying the gun down the back of my jeans waistband was quite an awesome experience. If you carry a gun you've got to be in the right mindset where if you're in a position where you have to draw your gun and use it then that's what you've got to do. A lot of people carry guns for show but are reluctant to use them. Wrong mindset. I was itching to take my gun to the gun club and get in some practice but I figured it wouldn't be a cool thing to turn up with an illegal gun and start blasting away.

My gun stayed in the flat in a bag with my knife, my C.S. gas, my money and my passport and any other valuables I had. That bag lived in a small cubby hole under the rug in the hallway to the flat which I had quick and easy access to if any of the surrounding Muslims decided to kick off. I kept my bicycle in the hallway so it wouldn't get stolen or sabotaged so if need be I could make my escape from the north part of Amsterdam back to the main part of the city and relative safety. Fortunately at the end of the day my precautionary measures weren't needed.

In August of nineteen ninety the 'Tall Ships' arrived in Amsterdam. They were here for two weeks. About twenty to thirty Tall Ships from around the world lined the quays of the harbour for all to view and visit. To get to work in the city I had to get the ferry across the harbour to behind the railway station. Normally an easy journey with little hazard but for two weeks with the ships in it became a hazardous and chaotic cruise. With small motor craft and yachts cruising up and down the river while we were trying to cross it I'm surprised there weren't any accidents but it was a fantastic sight to see.

Thousands of people crowded the harbour to marvel at the sight of these vast three and four mast ocean going sailing ships. I was no exception as were quite a lot of the other croupiers in town. Scottish Gerry and I took a boat tour around the harbour to get an even closer look at some of these monsters.

I was fortunate to witness them all set sail and one by one file out of the harbour with there sails flapping proudly in the breeze and the crew standing precariously on top of the masts. I was lucky to see them again four years later in Weymouth harbour.

A short while after the 'Tall Ships' event I was walking along the waters edge behind the railway station after a session at the gun club to catch a ferry home. It was dark and I was walking along the bicycle path when I happened to look behind me and I noticed this dark blue car slowly following me on the same bicycle path. Not knowing who they were or what they wanted I was, to say the least, a bit nervous. I was thinking 'who have I upset recently, is this a hit, is it the cops in plain clothes coming to bust me?' I wasn't going to run I just kept on walking, only a little faster.

I turned my head around to see what was going on and the car stopped. For a few seconds nothing happened then the car doors opened and four men climbed out of the car wearing balaclavas and black bomber jackets and started walking towards me. I was a bit worried, in fact I was shitting myself. I was unarmed, alone and there were four of them, big fuckers they were.

Suddenly they turned away from me and went down a slipway towards the water. I stood and watched, intrigued as to what was going on. A feeling of relief washing through me. Out of the darkness a small low motor boat with no lights pulled up at the end of the slipway and two men flashing police insignia dragged a handcuffed and blindfolded man out of the boat and handed him over to the waiting four men. Two of them got him by the arms and frogged marched him back to the car. They threw him in the back seat, started the engine, climbed the curb onto the road and drove off into the night. I went home. Nothing to do with me.

A few days later I was round at Gary's flat listening to some of his new demo tapes. Now that he had a good job as a music journalist he was always getting cassettes sent to him of new bands about to be released. We were listening to stuff before it hit the high street. Gary took a phone call from a friend of his. He looked over at me and asked if I fancied going to see Luciano Pavarotti that evening in Belgium. I said yes. Gary finished his conversation and put the phone down.

I was never into opera much but the BBC had used Pavarotti singing Nessum Dorma during the world cup in Italy and I'd really liked it. I'd found it quite moving. Later that day Gary's friend picked us up in his van with others in tow and he drove us all the way into Belgium for the concert. Leaving the others to take their seats Gary and I went up into the circle. It was quiet so we could wander round at will. We smoked joints and snorted cocaine off our hands and thoroughly enjoyed Luciano Pavarotti live on stage.

Gary was good at coming up with these little surprise jaunts. Earlier in the summer we'd got an invite to go and see the West Indian cricket team play the Dutch cricket team. It was a nice summer's day. We had plenty of cold cans of Heineken and ready rolled joints and along with the sound of reggae playing we got to watch Viv Anderson and his boys play cricket.

CHAPTER FIFTY
EXPLODING COCAINE

There was a whole bunch of us in The O'Porto bar. It must have been around November or December time because I knew that some of the boys had got their hands on some powerful firecrackers. With the beer flowing and the double vodkas disappearing just as quickly something was bound to happen and who'd have thought I'd be the instigator?

The boys were down the end of the bar by the toilets playing darts. I can remember that Brendan and Kenny were there along with Nobby. I was sat at the other end of the bar with Karen, Julie and Tracey by the entrance. In between throws at the dart board the boys were messing around and throwing each other into the toilet and holding the door closed so they couldn't get out. In particular they were ganging up on Nobby.

After awhile I noticed that Nobby was getting pissed off with being picked on and I noticed that Brendan was the main protagonist. So when Nobby approached the bar to get in a round of drinks I excused myself from the girls and sidled up to Nobby at the bar. Making sure no one heard me I said to Nobby "Here take this piece of chalk, go into the toilet crush it and cut two big fat lines on top of the toilet." Nobby looked at me with a blank expression on his face. So I explained "You know what Brendan's like for cocaine, tell him there's a couple of lines of coke in there for him. When he goes in take two of those firecrackers, light them and throw them in after him and hold the door shut." Nobby looked at me and a big knowing grin spread across his face.

A few minutes later there was a commotion down at the end of the bar. Brendan was seen entering the toilet quickly followed by two fizzing firecrackers and the door was being firmly held shut by Nobby and Kenny. Two loud explosions silenced the bar and smoke poured out from the gaps around the door and through the ceiling. Nobby and Kenny released the door and a shell shocked Brendan emerged. Nobby got a standing ovation from all the croupiers and we were all thrown out the bar. It was well worth it just to see Brendan's face and they didn't pick on Nobby again after that.

Christmas time came. I stocked up with plenty of good food, plenty of beers, a bottle of Remy Martin brandy and a bottle of scotch. I laid my hands on a couple of grams of coke and some hash and grass and spent a drunken hedonistic Christmas Day on my own.

New Years Eve was a more sociable event. Lang Marcel's mother owned a bar on one of the canals and Lange Marcel decided to throw a party for all his staff at the '217' and the rest of his gang. A buffet was laid on and countless bottles of champagne were available. Everybody had their own bottle of champagne and when that was empty we just went and got another one. As midnight approached it was time to get the fireworks out.

Lange Marcel had bought a fifty thousand piece firecracker. He didn't bother to string it up like most people he just laid it out along the canal and across the bridge. As the clocks throughout the city struck midnight Lange Marcel lit the blue touch paper and the night exploded in its usual manner. As the firecracker exploded closer to the bridge a stray burning ember flew into the cardboard box containing all the other fireworks and exploded in one all mighty big bang with bangs whizzes and rockets shooting out at all angles and casino staff diving in all directions. Another good New Years Eve in Amsterdam.

CHAPTER FIFTY ONE
SHARING A BED WITH TRACEY

New Years Day 1991, just another day. Still feeling the effects of the night before. All was normal, all was boring. Life continued with work and the pub crawls and the gun club. On the twenty eighth of February the war in the Gulf ended with Kuwait liberated and Saddam's forces surrendering in the thousands.

On the nineteenth of March I made my last trip to the gun club. Tommy was recruiting staff to go and work in Turkey and he asked me to join him. I fancied something different. I'd been in Amsterdam for ten years and jumped at the chance to work in a different country. I packed up my gear and stashed it in the attic round at Steve's. I passed my flat in the north onto a couple of croupiers and on the first of April I flew out of Amsterdam bound for Istanbul. Tommy had recruited staff from Holland and Germany and the flight over turned into a party as I re-acquainted myself with croupiers I hadn't seen for years. After a night in Istanbul we flew out east to a place called Adana where I worked for three months. I quit Adana and returned to Amsterdam via Crete.

I arrived back in the city homeless and jobless. I had a wad of money in my back pocket and I needed to find somewhere to stay while I got my act together. I had Tracey's phone number so I gave her a ring in the hope she could put me in touch with the old gang. Tracey invited me round so I hopped into a cab and went straight round to see her.

I paid the taxi, rang the bell and Tracey buzzed me in. I lugged my luggage up the thin narrow stairs to Tracey's flat where I was greeted with a hug and a kiss. She gave me a cold beer, rolled me a joint and cut me a line of coke. Tracey was always the perfect hostess. I told her I was looking for someone to put me up for a few days while I got myself sorted. She told me I could stay with her.

My eyes scanned round Tracey's perfectly decorated one roomed flat and settled on the settee. It wasn't too big but I said the settee would be fine. I could sleep anywhere if need be. Tracey said I didn't have to sleep on the settee I could share the bed with her, so I said o.k. It being a Sunday afternoon Tracey opened her freezer door and pulled out a leg of lamb and a joint of beef and asked me what I fancied for dinner. I chose the beef and she laid it on the side in the kitchen to defrost. Later that afternoon after a few beers and more joints I took a relaxing hot shower while Tracey rustled up a full on Sunday roast. After dinner I put my feet up and relaxed and told Tracey about my three months in Turkey and my long trek along the south coast of Turkey by bus to Marmaris.

Tracey was working the night shift somewhere in town. I would often be tucked up asleep when she came home but occasionally I would wake up and watch her strip down to her knickers before climbing into bed. One night it was thunder and lightening outside and Tracey cuddled up to me. She asked me how come I never came on to her in all the years we'd known each other. I told her that she had a reputation as a man-eater and I was never sure if I could live up to her expectations and that sexually she scared the shit out of me.

Whilst Tracey was sleeping and working I was out and about tracking down old friends, restoring my contacts and looking for work. Karen and Gary offered me their attic room to stay in so I accepted. The attic was a small room full of junk on the fifth floor with a single bed along one wall and a window leading out to a roof. I left the window open one night when I went to work and someone climbed through and robbed me. Fortunately my money and passport were well hidden. We knew it had to be someone local who lived in the same block of flats. Karen's flat was one of hundreds in a large oval shaped block. The ground floor flats all had gardens and the only access to this roof was through all these small attic windows.

One night Gary and I were sat downstairs from the flat by the canal under a Weeping Willow tree smoking hash and drinking a bottle of vodka fresh from the freezer. I threw the empty vodka bottle into the canal and we both swallowed a handful of psilocybin mushrooms. As the mushrooms took effect and it was a full moon I suggested to Gary we take a walk on the roof. We rolled a couple of joints before the mushrooms made us incapable and we went back inside and up to the attic and stepped through the window onto the roof.

It wasn't so much of a roof as a walkway which was about ten feet deep and ran the whole way around the inside of this vast block of flats. We both lit up a joint each and started walking. The moonlight reflected off the pebbles that lined the walkway which only added to the effect of the mushrooms. Occasionally we would walk up to the edge and peer down into the gardens below. At one stage we hid in the shadows as someone opened a window to see what the manic giggling was all about. It was a long walk but we went all the way round and finally climbed back into the attic window still drunk, still tripping and stoned.

A short while after moving out of Tracey's she decided to pack up and go back home to Newcastle. Joe, a friend of hers drove over in a van and I helped them both load the van up with her stuff. As I still hadn't found a job I made an on the spot decision to return to England with them and visit my mother in Bognor Regis. I rushed home and packed a bag and grabbed my passport while they finished up loading the van and we drove out of Amsterdam for the ferry back to England.

A few days later I was back in Amsterdam and I went to the '217' about getting my job back. Lang Marcel was out but Ronnie was in and he told me I couldn't get a job. A few days later I was back in the '217' and this time I spoke to Lange Marcel. He wasn't too pleased about the way I left and took off to Turkey and he wasn't too pleased with Ronnie for not giving me a job. So I was back in the '217' working for Lange Marcel again.

Lange Marcel had Big Pete working for him on the door. It was quite a sight one afternoon when Big Pete came into the casino from the door to see Lange Marcel. Along with Ronnie the three of them were stood in the middle of the floor having a conversation. It was like a meeting of giants. Big Pete was about eight feet tall, Lange Marcel was about seven feet tall and Ronnie was about six and a half feet tall. It was made more noticeable when one of the Indonesians walked by to say hello and had to crane his neck to look up.

Business must have been good. One afternoon Lange Marcel, Frans, Martin and Ronnie came walking down the casino floor four abreast. All four of them looked like gangsters. Lange Marcel had taken them out shopping and here they were all wearing brand new suits, shirts, ties and shoes. It was a weird sight as, apart from Ronnie who always wore a suit, the other guys usually wore denims.

One day out of the blue this guy called Raymond turned up. He was obviously connected to Lange Marcel because he headed straight for the office. Another tall Dutch man with shoulder length hair. He was a good looking guy but he had this dangerous aura about him which made me nervous. He had a big white vicious looking dog which he'd bring into the casino. One day he came in and let it off its lead. The dog had a quick sniff around then went up to this punter who had fallen asleep in a chair. He cocked its leg and pissed over this poor guy's leg. I tried to stay away from Raymond as much as I could.

During the summer I started seeing a lot more off Angie. I'd known Angie for years. She had big blue eyes, blond hair and a beautiful body. Angie loved her vodka and her cocaine. She had a room in the Corner House hotel so I would pop round to see her occasionally and we'd get drunk and wired. We had to keep our relationship quiet as she was still seeing her boyfriend at the time. We didn't even tell her friend Julie, though after a while I think she cottoned on.

After a few months Kirsten and Tommy returned from Turkey. The three of us were out one night with Chinese Dave. It was his birthday. We'd been out for a meal and we ended up in the Homolulu. It must have been mid week because when we entered the place was dead. There was the four of us, a couple of Chinese boys and two Turkish lads over by the restaurant area.

We took a booth along the side of the bar and got the drinks in. After a while I nipped off to the toilet for a line of cocaine. On the way out of the toilet and walking round the bar I heard one of the Chinese guys having heated words with the two Turks. When I got back to the booth I told Tommy there might be trouble. We continued drinking and I kept an eye on the potential trouble over in the corner.

As predicted it kicked off big style. The heated words turned into a full blown argument. One of the Turks pulled a knife and started stabbing one of the Chinese boys in the stomach. The other Chinese boy ran out to the cloakroom and came back in with a gun and promptly shot the Turk dead. By now they had our attention and when the other Turkish boy started running our way with the Chinese guy aiming his gun at him we all four of us ducked under the table. I was the last one under the table and before I went down I saw Kirsten's hand reach up and grab her drink.

The Turkish boy escaped through the door. We made the instant decision to depart the scene as well before the police arrived. So we grabbed our drinks and went out to the cloakroom where the doorman already had our coats ready. We put on our coats and as we left the

Homolulu the police were already pulling up in force. They saw us exiting the club with drinks in hand but did nothing to stop us so we kept walking and climbed into a taxi round the corner. We decided to go to the Corner House and on the way we saw the Chinese guy with the gun walking along by a canal.

We got to the Corner House and Kirsten, Tommy and Chinese Dave went inside. I made an excuse to linger back and when they couldn't see me I rang Angie's bell and went on up. I was buzzing, drunk, stoned and wired and told Angie what had just happened. Later during the night she reminded me that I'd already told her the story three times.

The next morning after spending the night with Angie I was downstairs in the hotel bar having some breakfast when I saw Chinese Andrew and Fang walk by. I went out to say hello to Andrew as he'd been away for awhile. I asked him when he'd got out and he told me he hadn't been released he'd done a runner. Crazy man, he only had another year to do. I didn't fancy being around Andrew if the police came calling as Andrew was likely to shoot it out with them if he was in a bad mood. I said a quick goodbye and went back inside to finish my breakfast.

As winter came upon us so did the risk of getting raided. Lange Marcel was expecting it. He got hold of a radio scanner which he installed on the reception so the doormen could listen into the police frequency. Occasionally I would venture out onto the streets and wander round the block searching for police cars and vans. I'd be on the look out for any unmarked cars with undercover cops taking photos of our entrance.

One time on one of my wanderings I noticed a junkie checking the doors of the cars parked alongside the casino. I went back in to tell the doormen, that would be one battered junkie. But instead Jerome decided to use me as a dumbbell and lifted me above his head half a dozen times. When he put me down I told him about the junkie but by the time he'd gone out the door the junkie was gone.

A couple of weeks later we did get raided. It was a quiet afternoon and the doormen gave us warning so I left the tables grabbed a drink and sat down at a table by the bar playing backgammon. There was no way out. Uniformed and plain clothes cops came steaming in guns drawn. Ronnie greeted them and the police started to search and arrest people. Once searched the punters were released. Those unlucky croupiers were arrested.

When it came to my turn I assumed the position against the wall and this copper frisked me. Turning me round he asked if I worked there. I told him I didn't. He said it was illegal to lie to a police officer. I insisted I didn't work there and told him I was a punter, showing him a handful of cash chips. He asked me where my coat tag was and I told him I was in and out all day and they knew my coat so I didn't have one. He didn't believe me. He took me out to reception where I retrieved my coat and he put my name into a computer to see if I was wanted elsewhere. Satisfied that I was o.k. he told me to stay on reception then he went back inside.

That was a silly move. I put my coat on and walked out of there trying to avoid contact with anyone. I walked up the side street and when I was out of sight I broke into a run and headed for O'Henry's bar. I ran into the bar, parked my ass at the bar and ordered a beer and a double scotch and told them I was on the run. After awhile I strolled back to the '217' to see what was going on. The police had gone and the casino was locked up. We'd been closed down and once again I was out of a job.

CHAPTER FIFTY TWO
1992

Ninety one drifted into ninety two in a forgotten blur. I'd got myself a small studio flat above a bar on the Raadhuisstraat opposite the Westerkerk. Next to the bar was a Spanish restaurant specialising in Paella. During the early part of the year I was suffering from a stinking cold and would often spend the night in the bar knocking back double Remy Martin's. Most of the bars in Amsterdam had this way of warming up the brandy glass using the steam produced from the coffee machine.

I managed to get a job working for Franz, one of the Germans in town. We were on the Nieuwendijk and we were only dealing blackjack. Franz was very rarely there as he had casinos all over Holland and Germany so he was always away on 'business'. Franz would do this thing where he would ring up his managers and tell them he would be in shortly to inspect the casino. This would get all the managers running around in a panic making sure everything was clean and spotless. One time he fired a waitress on the spot because when he walked into one of his casinos he found a solitary cigarette butt in an ashtray.

I was working with Hank again from the '88' days and his brother Rien. After I'd left the small studio flat on the Raadhuisstraat Hank fixed me up with a room at his mother's house for a short period. I'd been working for a few weeks and everything seemed to be o.k. We were busy and I was dealing blackjack one afternoon when Franz entered the casino. I'd never worked for Franz before, he didn't know me and I didn't know him. He asked his manager who the dealer with the ginger hair was. He told him and Franz had me fired on the spot. Apparently he thought people with ginger hair were unlucky. Tell that to all my previous bosses for the last eleven years.

Dominic, who had worked for Franz for years, thought he was out of order. Two days later I was back in the same casino working for him. Dominic had invented a new card game. He'd had some eminent professors of mathematics and statistics look into the odds and percentages of the game and Dominic had hired some space upstairs from Franz in order to get his game up and running to try and fine tune it. Dominic had a new cloth made for his new game and we fitted that to a blackjack table. He also had a blackjack table put in as well so we could at least try to make some money for us to survive while we experimented. It must have pissed Franz off to see me back in his casino but he couldn't do much about it as I was working for Dominic.

After awhile Dominic shut his two tables down as we weren't making enough money. Once again I was out of work so I took off to the Greek island of Zakynthos to visit my mother and sister who were tour reps out there for the summer. This is where I met Alison, a blue eyed, blonde tour rep who worked with my mother and sister.

When I returned to Amsterdam after about a month under the Greek sun Tommy got me a job working as a blackjack dealer for Freddy in the Femina on the Rembrandts Plein and I took a room in the

City Hotel right round the corner from the casino. We had an open door policy and it would seem the bosses were never worried about getting raided.

CHAPTER FIFTY THREE
BLACKJACK SHENANIGANS

It was whilst working with Tommy in the Femina that I continued my education when it came to dealing blackjack. I'd been dealing blackjack now for many years. I was quite good at it. I could deal with my eyes closed, which is what we used to do sometimes just to show off.

Back in 1984 I'd learnt the basics of card counting with Tommy and Steve in the 'Goldfish Bowl'. Several years later working with Tommy again he taught me some shifty moves with the cards which increased the house edge. He was taking his card counting skills and turning them around to give the house an advantage.

First he showed me the Hi-Low pick up. This involved picking up the used cards in a random fashion so that one low card was with a high card and vice versa. This move would give the punters a lot of 13's, 14's and 15's and decrease the likelihood of getting 20's and blackjacks. This move wasn't very subtle as it was done in plain sight of the punters. On the whole they were oblivious to what we were doing. Only those in the know knew what we were doing and if they didn't like it we told them to stop playing or take advantage of what we were up to.

Our next trick was to keep a track of the cards as they were dealt and to track the cards in the discard tray. With a bit of fancy subtle hand work the cards would be placed in the discard tray in such a way. The tens and picture cards would be kept together in the bottom of the tray. The small denomination cards would go in the middle of the discard tray and the aces would be placed on top of the smaller cards. When it came to shuffling the cards for the next shoe we would shuffle the small cards in with the tens and aces. This method would reduce the punter getting 20's and blackjacks and any split aces would end up with a 2, 3, 4 or 5. This method was a lot more subtle and we used it for many years.

When I worked with Tommy in the Femina he came up with another little move. When the dealer was holding an ace we would offer 'full' insurance on their bet. If they had a ten guilder bet then they could take a full ten guilder insurance bet. At odds of two too one they would actually win money if the dealer pulled a blackjack. We managed to get the insurance bet up to five hundred guilders regardless of their original bet and we would offer the bet to anyone in the casino whether they were playing or not. This bet eventually went up to a thousand guilders. Now some of you out there who are clued in must be thinking we were mad.

Not so. We had our own card up our sleeve and he was called Tommy. I would deal blackjack and Tommy would be my Inspector. What he was actually doing was counting the cards and keeping a side count of the tens and picture cards. When I was holding an ace Tommy would give me a coded word. One word would mean the remaining cards were rich in tens so I would offer insurance very quickly and quietly then pull my next card.

The other coded word would mean the remaining cards were rich in small cards and I would take my time offering insurance. We would get as many people as possible to take the bet and lay down their money. We would call out to the punters at the bar or playing roulette and remind them of our odds and maximum bets. They fell for it every time. The money would come flying in and I would almost certainly end up drawing a low card and raking in all those lost insurance bets. We made the house thousands from that little scam.

Psychology was another tool we would use to our advantage. Some punters you could just talk into making the wrong move like taking a card or doubling down or splitting their cards. Especially as we had control of the cards during the shuffle and we could track the cards during play.

I continued working at the Femina for the rest of 1992 then decided to take Christmas off. On the twenty-first of December I flew out to Cyprus to spend Christmas and New Year with Alison who I had met on Zakynthos in the summer.

CHAPTER FIFTY FOUR
MEETING LISA

On the fifth of January I flew out of Cyprus and returned to England. I hung out at my mothers for a few weeks then I got a call from Tommy asking me if I wanted to return to Turkey. I jumped at the chance and on the fifteenth of March I was flying out to a place called Kusadasi on the west coast of Turkey with Pete 'the prat with the hat'. I was there for three months and it was there where I hooked up with an Australian girl called Lisa who had been hired to look after Tommy and Kirsten's baby daughter Zara. Lisa was fired by Tommy after one too many drinking sessions with me and when I decided to quit Turkey Lisa came with me. So on the eleventh of June we flew back to Amsterdam via Frankfurt in Germany.

Back in Amsterdam through a friend I made contact with Joan. Joan had been in Amsterdam longer than I had. She used to work for Frans Diggelen when he owned the Hermes down on the Weteringschans. Joan lived on the Fannius Scholtenstraat and had an empty flat going upstairs from her and we moved in immediately. We were on the top floor. It had two bedrooms, a bathroom and a large kitchen/lounge area. It was a nice flat and we proceeded to make it our home.

Through Joan's connections I got a job working for Dieter. He'd just opened up the casino part in the Queens Club. The Queens Club was owned by Frans Diggelen. It consisted of a Mah Jong area leading into a restaurant, which wasn't being used. Upstairs from the restaurant was a bar which mainly catered for the Japanese businessmen in the city and next to that but behind secured double doors was the casino. It was a small place which held two blackjack tables, an American roulette table and a poker table.

Out of the three Germans that operated in Amsterdam Dieter was the more laid back and understood the gambling business. He owned a string of casinos and had several bookies in Germany so he had more of an understanding and respect for odds and percentages. He was still a German though and although he liked me I didn't want to give him an excuse to fire me. I remember one time when it was the anniversary of the Dresden fire bombing in WW2 he asked one of the younger English croupiers what they thought about it. Them being young didn't know what he was talking about. I knew what he was on about and was glad he didn't ask for my opinion as my grandfather was a Squadron Leader on that particular mission.

We did good business and we settled into a nice routine. Big Henk came in one night and dropped twenty five thousand guilders. I got the usual verbal attack from him calling me all the names under the sun. I must have impressed Dieter because after Henk left he came up to me and told me he liked the way I handled myself. I told Dieter I'd known Henk for years and was used to it. As I put it to him 'every time Henk swears at me it costs him a grand.' He liked that attitude.

I got to know Frans Diggelen a lot better as he was still running the bar next door. Through Joan's connection with Frans, Lisa got a part time job working for him. Frans needed someone to do some basic light housework, wash his clothes and iron them. Frans had always been a perfectionist and after explaining to Lisa how he liked his clothes to be hung and put away to his required specifications he showed Lisa his iron and ironing board. Lisa told him his equipment was old and needed updating so he immediately went out and bought her everything new.

So with me working full time and Lisa bringing in some money for herself we settled in to living and working in Amsterdam. I showed her the sights and introduced her to my old friends in the city. I introduced her to the concept of 'Monday night shopping' which she thought was great. Every first Monday of the month when everyone threw out their unwanted items we would trawl the neighbourhood streets to see what we could find. One night we came across this big overflowing box of English written books. There was fiction and non-fiction so we both got searching through them and putting aside those we wanted to take home. With Lisa's head buried deep inside this box a police patrol car pulled up along side us and asked what we were doing. Thinking nothing of it I explained and they told us that it wasn't our property so we should leave it alone. We walked away from there around a corner. When they drove off we went back and collected what we had put aside.

Kirsten and Tommy returned from Turkey with Zara so we put them up for a few days. Kirsten's temper was on a short fuse and when she had an argument with Tommy she would threaten to take a pair of scissors to his clothes and stab him in the back with them. Being good friends and loyal to them both I felt I was in an awkward position so when their arguments got really bad Lisa and I would go out and leave them to it. But it was nice having them around.

Christmas came and while Lisa busied herself making decorations for the flat I went out and bought a Christmas tree. I went to the Haarlemmer Plein just up the road from us and checked out the guys selling Christmas trees. I settled for this one tree for twenty-five guilders and took it home. Lisa was expecting something small. This thing was a foot higher than our ceiling so I had to cut the top off.

We had a good Christmas and I introduced Lisa to the delights of spending New Years Eve in Amsterdam and we slipped into nineteen ninety-four.

CHAPTER FIFTY FIVE
HERE, THERE AND EVERYWHERE

At the beginning of 1994 Dieter closed down his operation in the Queens Club. I wasn't to be out of work for long though as he offered Joan and myself a job in one of his casinos in the south of Holland. There wasn't a lot of work going in Amsterdam and as I now had Lisa to support and make sure the rent was paid I accepted his offer.

Joan drove me down to the casino in this quiet clean non-descript town down in the south. Like Loosdrecht, the sort of place you just couldn't imagine there being a casino. During the week when we were working Joan and I stayed in this modern motel. Small, clean compact rooms where even the showers were coin operated. We found a couple of nice restaurants so we ate well and there were a couple of bars to hang out in. On our days off we would drive back to Amsterdam. I got to see Lisa and Joan got to take care of her flat.

The casino was situated in the basement of a building. It was quite a large place with four blackjack tables. I impressed Dieter one night by catching this guy out trying to pass a forged thousand guilder note. After a couple of months the casino was raided and shut down so we returned to Amsterdam.

All was not gloom and doom as I was soon offered a job by Brendan. He was working for this German guy in Germany at a place called Wurzburg. Kenny had been working there but got caught stealing money and was fired. It was a simple set up. I would work for two weeks then Brendan would work for two weeks. I travelled down with Brendan so he could show me the ropes.

We stayed in a small hotel and I soon found out about the scam that he and Kenny were operating. The boss didn't want thousand deutschmark notes putting down the drop box. What we were supposed to do was take the note to the boss who would exchange it for ten one hundred deutschmark notes. As we were both responsible for the one blackjack table that was operating we had no one observing us so we would wait until we had two thousand deutschmark notes and then we would change them up. Only between the table and the boss one of those notes would disappear into either mine or Brendan's pockets. We could make an extra five hundred to a thousand deutschmarks a night between us.

With the place being so busy Brendan stayed on and my allotted two weeks turned into thirty days straight without a day off. I wasn't complaining the money was rolling in. On the thirty first day I returned to Amsterdam for a much needed two weeks off with a pocket full of several thousand deutschmarks.

A couple of days later there was a knock at the door and it was Brendan. He should have been in Wurzburg awaiting my return. Brendan told me that the casino had been raided and shut down. This was in Germany remember not Holland. He explained how as it was quiet he was playing on one of the slot machines when suddenly men in black with balaclavas and machine pistols came bursting through the door and windows SAS style. Brendan was taken in, questioned and released. He was a bit pissed of though. He went back to the casino the next day and the slot machine he was playing on with all his money in it that was ready to pay out had been confiscated by the German police.

At the time it wasn't such a hardship being out of work again as I had a pocket full of deutschmarks. Fortunately Joan came through again and Dieter offered us both a job in Dusseldorf. So once again I was leaving home for work and again crossing the border into Germany.

We were working in the city centre in a place that had at one time been a corner shop of some description. The windows were blacked out and in the front part were several tables laid out for playing cards and Backgammon. In the back room behind a closed door were a couple of blackjack tables. Dieter had a partner called Hans. He was a big strong looking jovial local German who had a string of 'businesses' in the city. As I only had only one day off a week I didn't go back to Amsterdam but enjoyed myself exploring the nightlife of a busy German city.

I had been there for about six weeks when one night this crazy Chinese guy kicked off big style. He was ejected but threatened to come back with a gun and start shooting people. This wasn't a good situation because through experience I knew the Chinese usually carried out their threats. The doors were locked, the tables were closed down and secured and we just sat around playing cards and drinking coffee. We were also expecting a raid so I couldn't understand why we were just sat around waiting for something to happen. I told Joan we should leave and go back to the hotel but she said to sit tight and wait.

After about an hour the doorbell rang. The doorman answered it and let the same Chinese guy back in. He spoke to Dieter and Hans and everything was calmed down and we opened up again, but I wasn't happy with the situation. Later that night back at the hotel I spoke to Joan. I expressed my opinion about working in a place which seemed to have very little security where they let a mad Chinese guy who had threatened to shoot people back into the casino. I told her I'd made up my mind to quit and go back to the safety of Amsterdam.

The next night I spoke to Dieter and Hans and told them I was going. Hans took me out for a drink to try to persuade me to stay. He took me to one of his nightclubs just round the corner. It was a pole dancing club with half naked girls dancing all over the place. He told me he liked me and he liked my work and he said if I stayed I could come here to his club on my nights off and enjoy myself on the house. It was a tempting offer but I'd made up my mind and the next day I caught the train back to Amsterdam.

As it was nearing the end of the year and there was no work around Lisa and I decided to give up the flat and go back home to stay with my mother who was now living in Weymouth.

CHAPTER FIFTY SIX
THE QUEEN'S CLUB

I wasn't earning enough money in England to survive so leaving Lisa at home with my mother I returned to Amsterdam in the spring of 1995. With little money in my pocket I needed somewhere to stay. Leslie offered me her spare bedroom so I gratefully accepted. She lived far out of the city centre which meant I had to travel by underground to get to her place.

With Dieter gone Frans had reopened the Queens Club casino with some Chinese partners. Frans gave me a job and after a couple of weeks I noticed that there was conflicting styles of operating between Frans and the Chinese. Eventually it all came to a stand-off between them and the Chinese left. The Chinese wanted me to go with them but I decided to stay with Frans. Before the Chinese left though they wanted their ten thousand guilders front money they had put up to open. Things weren't looking good for Frans who refused to pay them. I thought at one stage they might shoot him but finally the situation got sorted out and now Frans was in sole charge of his own club and he made me his manager. Before I started working for Frans I took the weekend off and flew back to England to see Lisa.

So after fourteen years of working in Amsterdam and building up a good reputation I was finally elevated to the grand position of 'casino manager'. This meant I got to wear a suit and tie and hang out in the bars and look important with the other managers in town. It was all an ego thing, but fun.

I owned two suits, both dodgy. One was a shiny gray suit which wouldn't have looked out of place on Miami Vice. The other one was a wool blue pin stripe suit which I'd picked up for one pound at a jumble sale on my last trip to England. The tie I bought to go with it cost me ten pence. Tommy was impressed, he wanted to give me five pounds and get Lisa to go out and get him five.

I had two blackjack tables, one American roulette table, and a Caribbean Poker table under my control. We had a poker table in the window but it was never used. I had six croupiers, a couple of waitresses and my friend Wayan was in the cash desk. We were busy, too busy. Frans wanted the club to be more upmarket and we were getting a lot of the Surinamers coming in, spending little and just hanging around drinking and eating for free. One day I had about a dozen of them on the premises making the place look something like the old Mata Hari so I decided to act. I waited for them to get up and leave and I followed them down to reception. I got them all together and told them they were barred and not to come back. They didn't like it and the old women reached into their handbags and pulled out their knives for effect and told me they would get me.

With the riff-raff gone we settled down to attracting a better clientele. We had two Surinam ladies who were regulars. They were high rollers so they got to stay. One of them was evil. I'm sure she was some sort of a black witch but I always made her welcome. Her friend was a lot nicer and better looking. She was a big woman as in the sense of being tall and solidly put together if you know what I mean. Her upper thighs were as thick as a small tree trunk but I thought she was hot and she would often smother me in her more than ample chest.

Frans had a nice touch of making his customers feel appreciated. If we had some decent punters round the blackjack table he would appear with a plate of freshly cut fruit for them. Other times with some of our elder clientele he would nip next door to the bar and come back with a bottle of Sherry and some glasses and give them all a drink.

The Rolling Stones were due to play in Amsterdam sometime in late May. As I'd never seen the Stones live I wanted to go. Frans told me that as his manager I had to be at the Casino at all times but he eventually gave in and told me he would organise a couple of tickets for me. He told me he had the right connections and I believed him. He might have had the right connections but I never saw any tickets so the night the Stones rocked Amsterdam I was busy working.

One day I got Frans to show me the top floor of the club. It was a large space going back the full length of the building. Strewn across the floor collecting dust was a mish mash of items belonging to Frans' business downstairs. Chips, cards and old table cloths from the Casino. Bar attachments and old lights from the night club. Kitchen furniture and utensils and other fixtures and fittings from the restaurant.

At the time Frans had the casino up and running along with his night club next door. The restaurant was big with a fully fitted kitchen but not in use. Along the corridor leading into the restaurant there were eight small cubicles with sliding doors once used by the Japanese for playing Mah Jong. Each cubicle had an internal telephone connecting them to the bar and restaurant so they could order food and drink.

The potential was there for a thriving business with a captive audience. We were already catering for the high rollers in the casino. The bar was ticking over quietly but could do with some work to increase business. I suggested to Frans that he re-open the restaurant and make use of all the facilities at his finger tips. As for the space on the top floor I suggested we open it up as a high class brothel.

How could we go wrong? A casino, a restaurant, a nightclub and a brothel all on the same premises. Frans liked the idea, but there was a 'but'. Frans reckoned the authorities might not approve of us setting up a brothel in the same premises as what was still an illegal casino. He thought it might draw too much heat and get the whole lot closed down. So that put the kibosh on that little idea.

Over the years whenever Herman Brood was in town he would always do a gig at The Paradiso. If I wasn't working I would be there for a good dose of Dutch Rock 'n' Roll. Herman Brood was Holland's answer to Lou Reed. A fucked up junkie rock 'n' roller. You know the sort, a bottle of Jack Daniels in one hand and a syringe in the other. He was loud, he was raw, he was great.

Herman liked to play roulette and I got to know him when he started coming into the Queens Club. He came in one night and he stood there in front of me jumping up and down on one cowboy booted foot saying "Check out the socks Red, check out the socks." I checked out the socks. They were green but on closer inspection I noticed they were patterned after the layout of a roulette table. I asked him where he'd got them from. He said he couldn't remember but when he did he'd get me a pair.

Herman was getting into his art. Not collecting but painting and he had an exhibition in one of the small galleries in town. So one day I went down to see for myself. There was this one painting on canvas of different textures of cloth hanging over a screen. I liked it but when I enquired about the price I decided I didn't have ten thousand guilders lying about to purchase it. What a shame.

I was having trouble with a couple of my dealers. They were a young couple and they were always coming in about ten minutes late. I got the pair of them together one night and asked them why they were always late. They told me that every time they left to drive to work the canal bridge would go up at the same time every night to allow the boats through. I told them to either leave for work earlier or take a different route because if they were late again I would fire the pair of them. They were never late again.

Jerry was back in town from his tour in Turkey so I gave him a job. Frans and Jerry were old friends but Frans wasn't too pleased with Jerry working for him. I never understood why. Jerry worked for me for two weeks. He was dealing Caribbean Poker and doing his brains. Frans came up to me and said "Red, when he's finished giving away all my money fire him." So unfortunately I had to sack him.

Another friend of Frans' would come into the casino. He was an Indian called Ahmed. He was a big man with a big personality but he was a poor loser so Frans had barred him from playing the table's years ago in the Hermes. When he popped in for a visit he would always liven the place up. He came in one night quite late and placed a bottle of Johnny Walker Blue Label Whisky on the poker table and just left it there.

When we had closed and I'd done the count and everybody had gone home Frans and Ahmed were still sat at the poker table with the bottle of whisky in front of them. Ahmed told me he'd just come back from somewhere out East and he'd bought the bottle for me. Frans went next door to the bar and came back with three glasses. We opened the bottle, rolled some joints and snorted lots of cocaine. It all ended up, after some persuasion from Ahmed, next door in the bar singing a very drunken 'I did it my way' by Frank Sinatra on the karaoke machine.

All was well and I was enjoying being a Casino manager. One night things were going very badly. It was getting to the stage where my pay outs would exceed the amount of money I was holding on the premises. Not a good position to be in. A couple of months previous Frans had bought in a large fat sealed brown envelope with twenty five thousand guilders in it. He secured it in the safe telling me it was there for emergencies. That 'emergency' had just arrived so I went into the cash desk and opened it up. The envelope was full of paper not money. I called Wayan into the cash desk and showed him the envelope full of paper. I was livid.

I phoned Frans immediately, had a rant and a rave at him and told him I was doing my brains and needed more funds. He told me to cope as best I could and anyone not getting paid out would be sorted out the next day. At the end of the night I managed to pay everyone out except one. She just happened to be my friend the evil black witch. I wasn't looking forward to explaining the situation to her. She wasn't happy with the situation but after staring daggers at me she went quietly and came back the following day to get settled up.

That next day I had a big argument with Frans about the position he'd put me in and how it had affected the casinos reputation. Frans told me the envelope was there to test my honesty and loyalty. That really pissed me off so I told Frans I was quitting and I picked up my coat and walked out the Queens Club for good.

My ability to make sudden rash decisions along with my pride, ego and principles once more put me out of work. The next day I was on a plane flying back to England and home to Lisa.

CHAPTER FIFTY SEVEN
LAST THREE SPINS

In April of nineteen ninety six I was back in Amsterdam seeking fortune, I already had the fame. Lisa was at home at the flat with the cats in England and I was once again living out of a suitcase. I checked into the City Hall hotel on the Utrechtsestraat and went in search of work.

I wandered around the city checking out the usual bars where I was likely to find who was left in the city. I walked into the 'High Times' bar on the edge of the Red Light district. Nothing had changed much. Upstairs playing the pinball machine I found Brendan, Chinese Dave, Shortlegs and Kenny. Drinking beer, smoking joints and playing pinball. They were doing this when I left last time. I learnt that there wasn't a lot of work around but Brendan suggested I go and see Jerry who was still working at the Femina.

I left them to it and walked over to the Corner House. Sat outside at one of the tables I found Clark and Lynn having a drink. I got in a round of drinks and joined them. Clark and Lynn were working for a German crew round the corner from the Rembrandts Plein. Clark gave me the address and told me to come to the casino at nine o'clock and he'd put in a word for me.

Leaving them to finish their drinks I went to 'Smokey's' bar and coffee shop on the Rembrandts Plein. Here I found Justin and Amy along with Karen. Over a drink I told them I had a chance of getting a job and Karen offered me a bed at her place while I got myself sorted out. She gave me her phone number and I nipped along to the Femina to let Jerry know I was back in town.

Back at the City Hall hotel I showered and changed. I grabbed a bite to eat and at nine o'clock I went to see Clark at the casino. The casino was on the first floor above a Chinese restaurant called the 'Peking' on the Herengracht. Inside I met Clark and he spoke to one of the German bosses. There were four of them. All clean cut and smartly dressed. I didn't know any of them. I did a quick table test and got a job.

The casino was one large room. It was very clean and tidy and down one wall was about half a dozen windows overlooking the Vijzelstraat. There were two blackjack tables, an American roulette table, a small Craps table and a full size Baccarat table. I was due to start work the next night so with relief at landing myself a job I went out to explore the city, have a few drinks and see who else was left in Amsterdam.

The city was quiet and I didn't find anyone else. I decided to make the Homolulu my last port of call before going back to the hotel for a well earned sleep. It was at the Homolulu that I bumped into Dominic and Tracey. Dominic was his usual laid back self and was working in the Femina. Tracey had herself recently returned to Amsterdam with her new born daughter and had a nice large flat on the outskirts of the city. I took Tracey's address and after a few drinks and a gossip I went back to the hotel and slept.

I was woken at 11:45 a.m. by a knocking at my door. I swung my feet round onto the floor and sat there holding my head. For the first time in years I had a hangover, my head was throbbing and there was still a banging at my door. I lit a cigarette and opened the door. It was Jerry looking all cheerful with a big grin on his face. I splashed my face with some cold water, brushed my teeth, got dressed and we went out to grab a bite to eat. With a good old Dutch breakfast inside me I felt a little more human.

The Sun was up and it was a nice day so we headed for the Vondel Park. We strolled through the park, my hangover making the going tough as I tried to hold a conversation with Jerry. We rested up by a small muddy ditch and smoked a joint. The sound of dogs barking rattled my brain. I was feeling very stoned. The spring trees looked great with their new colourful budding leaves. The sun was hot and burning so we wandered on in search of a cold drink.

At one of the cafe's we both got ourselves a cold can of coke and sat on the grass watching some girls slip into roller blades and padded protection. After a while we realised that this guy was hiring them out and taking them on a rolling tour of the park. We got to thinking. We could get two groups of eight out every half an hour for an hour's tour at say fifteen guilders an hour, say ten groups a day that's approximately twenty four hundred guilders a day. That sort of money got us very excited and woke us both up a bit.

We watched the girls roll off on their tour and we parked our asses by a warm tree and watched the world go by. Eventually it was time to leave the park. We went back into the city and found a bar. We shot a couple of frames of Pool and played a few games of backgammon. I phoned Karen and arranged to move into her place the following day. Jerry and I went to grab a bite to eat then I went back to the hotel and sorted myself out for work that evening.

The casino was very quiet. During the evening we must have had about three or four punters come in. Very slow and boring but at least I was earning. For most of the shift we spent playing Texas Hold'em poker round the Baccarat table amongst ourselves. After work I went back to the hotel to get some much needed sleep. Later in the day I packed my bags, paid my hotel bill and got a taxi to Karen's flat on the Jan Hanzenstraat in the old west part of the city. Karen had two sons and I was sharing a bedroom with her eldest. He took the top bunk and I took the lower bunk. Karen had been working in Amsterdam for as long as I had if not longer. She was from the north part of England with big dark eyes and thick curly black hair.

Working in the casino was extremely dull and boring. It was so quiet I wondered if anyone knew it was there at all. I was playing more poker than actually dealing on the tables. We had a few high rollers come in and drop some serious money. If it wasn't for them I don't think we'd have stayed open for as long as we did.

When I wasn't working I was out and about in the bars having a drink and a joint with the few remaining croupiers that were left in town. The thrill and the excitement of those early days were long gone and now the city had lost its appeal and work was just a chore that was putting money in my pocket.

I stayed at Karen's for a month then Joan arranged a flat for me on the Joan Melchior Kemperstraat just round the corner from our old flat on the Fannius Scholtenstraat. It was a nice flat with a living room and a small bedroom with a kitchen and a bathroom. It was nice to have my own space again. Lisa came over to visit me a couple of times and it was on her last visit that I decided to call it a day and make plans to leave Amsterdam for good.

With Lisa back in England I was ringing her every day. Every other day I was getting a letter from her. We were both missing each other so plans were made for my return home. Lisa was going to start looking for a job in a hospital in a seaside town that had at least two casinos so I would be assured of a job on my return. I'd also come up with an idea to open a private poker club in England and with my guidance Lisa wrote off to the Gaming Board to gather as much information as possible for another of my crazy schemes. If I was going to go back home I was going to go straight. While these plans were being implemented I would stay working for as long as necessary and save as much money as I could.

Years ago in 1980 when I was working with Terry in Sheffield we had this new trainee called Simon. He was as camp as they come. Imagine a camp 'no more bets please' nice and loud throughout the casino. Well here I was in 1996 in a casino when I suddenly hear this very camp 'no more bets please' coming from this roulette table. I couldn't believe it Simon had arrived in town.

July dragged into August. Lisa had found a position going in a hospital in Plymouth on the south coast of England and she was confident of getting the job. As my departure from Amsterdam seemed imminent I left my flat and moved back into the City Hall hotel.

One night Big Dick came in at midnight. He played some roulette then a bit of blackjack and had a go on the Craps table. Then he went back on the roulette table and then on the blackjack. He did this for twenty three hours non stop. It was the longest shift I'd ever worked.

At eleven p.m. the following evening Big Dick finally left with empty pockets and a scowl. Fresh dealers were bought in and Clark, Lynn and I got paid and we went home. First I went to the night shop and bought a bottle of whisky, some beers and some much needed hot food. Back at the hotel I ate, had a drink and took a nice steaming hot shower. I put on some clean clothes and then went out to a party near Joan's until the small hours of the morning where I made the final decision to quit Amsterdam. The following day at work I told the boss I wanted a week off to go to England. It was granted and I told Clark I wouldn't be back but not to say anything and at the end of the week to give my job to Simon who had just lost his job.

September the first 1996. Eight o'clock in the morning. The sun is already shining brightly promising a glorious summer's day. My hotel bill is paid. My bags sit in the corner of the bar that I'm in. I'd just finished breakfast and was having a few farewell drinks and a couple of joints with some of the other croupiers that had just finished work. I went into the toilet and finished off my remaining cocaine. I paid my bar bill, grabbed my bags and crossed the square to get a taxi. Destination, Schipol airport.

So here I was, stoned and coked, sat in a taxi with the sun burning into my eyes listening to 'Shine on you crazy diamond' by Pink Floyd making my final exit from the city which had become home for fifteen years. There was no sadness, more like relief to be finally escaping. I'd had a good run over the years and now had a whole new life in front of me.

THE END

Printed in Great Britain
by Amazon